Object-Oriented Class Cohesion Measurement

Jehad Al Dallal

ISBN 978-1-7779025-0-6

Contents

Preface 7
About the Author 11
Chapter 1: Class Modeling 13
1.1. Graph-Based Class Models 13
1.1.1. Direct Method-Method Connectivity Graph 13
1.1.2. Indirect Method-Method Connectivity Graph 14
1.1.3. Method-Attribute Connectivity Graph 15
1.2. Matrix-Based Class Models 16
1.2.1. Direct Method-Attribute Matrix 16
1.2.2. Indirect Method-Attribute Matrix 16
1.2.3. Direct Method Invocation Matrix 18
2.2.4. Indirect Method Invocation Matrix 20
1.2.5. Direct Attribute-Type Matrix 20
1.2.6. Indirect Attribute-Type Matrix 21
2.2.7. Direct Parameter-Type Matrix 23
1.2.8. Indirect Parameter-Type Matrix 23
Summary 25
Chapter 2: Cohesion Measures 27
2.1. Use of Attribute/Type Measures 28
2.1.1. Coh 28
2.1.2. $LCOM_H$ 28
2.1.3. CAMC 29

2.2. Share of Attribute/Type Measures 30

2.2.1. $LCOM_{CK1}$ 30

2.2.2. $LCOM_{CK2}$ 31

2.2.3. TCC 32

2.2.4. LCC 33

2.2.5. DC_D 36

2.2.6. DC_I 37

2.2.7. CC 38

2.2.8. SCOM 39

2.2.9. LSCC 40

2.2.10. NHD 42

2.2.11. MMAC 43

2.3. Graph-Connectivity Measures 44

2.3.1. $LCOM_L$ 45

2.3.2. $LCOM_{HM}$ 45

2.3.3. CBMC 46

2.3.4. ICBMC 47

2.3.5. OL_n 50

2.3.6. PCCC 52

Summary 58

Chapter 3: Cohesion Measure Properties 59

3.1. Class Cohesion Measure Properties 59

3.2. Satisfaction to Measure Properties 60

3.2.1. Coh 60

3.2.2. $LCOM_H$ 62

3.2.3. CAMC 62

3.2.4. $LCOM_{CK1}$ 63

3.2.5. $LCOM_{CK2}$ 64

3.2.6. TCC 65

3.2.7. LCC 65

3.2.8. DC_D 66

3.2.9. DC_I 67

3.2.10. CC 68

3.2.11. SCOM 69

3.2.12. LSCC 70

3.2.13. NHD 72

3.2.14. MMAC 73

3.2.15. $LCOM_L$ 75

3.2.16. $LCOM_{HM}$ 76

3.2.17. CBMC 77

3.2.18. ICBMC 79

3.2.19. OL_n 80

3.2.20. PCCC 81

Summary 82

Chapter 4: Advanced Topics 85

4.1. Accounting for Cohesion Measure Applicability 85

4.1.1. Motivation 85
4.1.2. Assigning Cohesion Values 87
4.1.3. Empirical Validation 99
4.1.4. Summary 102
4.2. Accounting for Data Encapsulation in Cohesion Measurement 104
4.2.1. Motivation 104
4.2.2. Attribute/Parameter Weight Assignment Algorithm 106
4.2.3. Extended Class Cohesion Measures 108
4.2.4. Empirical Analysis for the Cohesion Values 110
4.2.5. Summary 126
4.3. Accounting for Special Methods in Cohesion Measurement 128
4.3.1. Motivation 128
4.3.2. Cohesive Relations of Special Methods 129
4.3.3. Qualitative Analysis 131
4.3.4. Empirical Analysis for the Cohesion Values 143
4.3.5. Summary 153
Bibliography 157
Index 165

PREFACE

A central goal of software engineering is to create techniques and tools that help developers build high-quality software—systems that are stable, reliable, and easy to maintain. To evaluate and improve software quality during development, developers and project managers use a variety of measures. For these measures to be useful, their results must accurately reflect the properties being assessed; otherwise, they can lead to poor design choices.

Software quality attributes are usually divided into **external** and **internal** categories. **External quality attributes** describe how the software performs from a user or operational perspective—factors that cannot be measured just by looking at the code or design documents. Examples include adaptability, reusability, understandability, maintainability, testability, and completeness.

- *Adaptability* refers to how easily software can be adjusted to run in new environments.
- *Reusability* reflects how easily components can be used again in other systems.
- *Understandability, maintainability, and testability* describe how easily a system can be understood, modified, and tested.

Measuring these external attributes usually requires observing the software in use or in its operational environment. For example, we can only measure maintainability after performing maintenance activities, and we can only measure reusability after the software has actually been reused. Because it is difficult to predict how often a component will be reused or how much future maintenance will cost, external quality attributes are often challenging to measure directly.

Internal quality attributes, such as size, coupling, and cohesion, are different. They can be measured directly from the software artifacts themselves—by examining the source code, design, or structure. While these internal measures do not directly describe how users experience the software, they are valuable because they can serve as indicators of external quality. For instance, higher cohesion and lower coupling often suggest better maintainability and understandability. Researchers also use internal measures to build predictive models of external quality, sometimes applying machine learning techniques to do so.

In object-oriented systems, the **class** is the main design unit. Each class encapsulates a set of attributes (data) and methods (behavior). The **cohesion** of a class expresses how closely related its members are. A class with high cohesion tends to be easier to understand, test, and maintain than one with low cohesion. **Class cohesion measures** aim to quantify this relatedness among a class's methods and attributes.

Many cohesion measures have been proposed to evaluate classes at different stages of design. High-level design (HLD) cohesion measures can identify potential cohesion problems early, even when detailed method-attribute interactions are not yet defined. Low-level design (LLD) cohesion measures make use of more detailed information available later in the design process. In these measures, an interaction between a method and an attribute—such as a method referencing an attribute—is typically treated as a sign of cohesion.

In this book, a comprehensive examination of object-oriented class cohesion measurement is presented. The book aims to clarify the theoretical foundations of class cohesion, provide an in-depth understanding of existing cohesion measures, and critically evaluate their validity and applicability. It is designed for researchers, software engineers, and graduate students interested in software quality assessment and measurement theory.

Chapter 1 introduces the fundamental models used to represent class members and their interactions. It explains how class cohesion can be modeled using graph-based and matrix-based representations, each capable of capturing both direct and indirect interactions between methods and attributes. The chapter also discusses how these models can express method-method interactions through invocations, and method-attribute interactions through attribute references, including cases involving attribute or parameter types.

Chapter 2 presents twenty established class cohesion measures, each derived from one of the models described in Chapter 1. These measures are grouped into three main categories according to their measurement approach: those that consider the use of attributes or types, those that focus on the sharing of attributes or types, and those based on graph connectivity concepts. Practical examples are included to demonstrate how each measure can be applied in assessing class cohesion.

Chapter 3 evaluates the theoretical validity of the considered cohesion measures by examining their compliance with essential cohesion properties.

Chapter 4 discusses advanced topics related to cohesion measurement. These include the assessment of measure applicability, the consideration of data encapsulation effects, and the treatment of special methods in cohesion analysis. These topics extend the discussion beyond theoretical and empirical validity and contribute to a deeper understanding of how cohesion measures perform in realistic software engineering contexts.

Together, these chapters provide a systematic exploration of class cohesion measurement — from foundational modeling concepts to advanced considerations. The book as a whole aims to guide readers toward both a conceptual understanding and a critical appreciation of how class cohesion can be effectively measured and interpreted in object-oriented software systems.

ABOUT THE AUTHOR

Prof. Jehad Al Dallal is a Professor in the Computer Science Department at the Gulf University for Science and Technology (GUST). He received his PhD in Computer Science from the University of Alberta in Canada, in 2003, where he was awarded the best Ph.D. researcher award. Prof. Al Dallal has led and contributed to numerous research projects in the areas of machine learning, generative AI, software testing, software metrics, and software refactoring. In addition, he has published more than 130 papers in conference proceedings and journals, including those of ACM, IEEE, IET, Elsevier, Wiley. According to the Stanford-Elsevier 2024 global ranking, he is listed among the top 2% of scientists worldwide. In 2025, he received the Distinguished Faculty Research Award from the Gulf University for Science and Technology in recognition of his outstanding scholarly contributions. Prof. Al Dallal was involved in developing more than 20 software systems. He also served as a technical committee member of several international conferences and as an associate editor for multiple peer-reviewed journals.

CHAPTER 1
CLASS MODELING

Researchers considered different models to represent the data of a class and their relationships considered in measuring cohesion. These models have different abstraction levels and they mainly can be classified into graph-based models and matrix-based models.

1.1. Graph-Based Class Models

1.1.1. Direct Method-Method Connectivity Graph

Direct Method-Method Connectivity (DMMC) graph is an undirected graph that consists of nodes and undirected edges. Each node represents a method in the class of interest and each edge represents the sharing of at least one attribute. In this graph, an edge connecting two nodes indicates a direct cohesive interaction between the two methods represented by the two nodes. The graph does not consider the indirect relationship between methods due to method invocation.

Example 1.1

The Java code given in Figure 1.1 shows an example class that has three methods and two attributes. Figure 1.2 shows the DMMC graph of the class. The graph has three nodes representing the three methods. Both methods m1 and m2 share the reference (i.e., definition or use) of attribute a1. This share of attribute a1 is represented by the undirected edge connecting nodes m1 and *m2*.

1.1.2. Indirect Method-Method Connectivity Graph

Indirect Method-Method Connectivity (IMMC) graph is an undirected graph that consists of nodes and undirected edges. Each node represents a method in the class of interest and each edge represents either the sharing of at least one attribute or the invocation of a method. In this graph, an edge connecting two nodes indicates a direct or indirect cohesive interaction between the two methods represented by the two nodes.

```
class Example_1 {
        int a1;
        int a2;
        void m1(){
                a1=1;
        }
        void m2(){
                a2=a1;
        }
        void m3(){
                m2();
        }
}
```

Figure 1.1. Java class *Example_1*

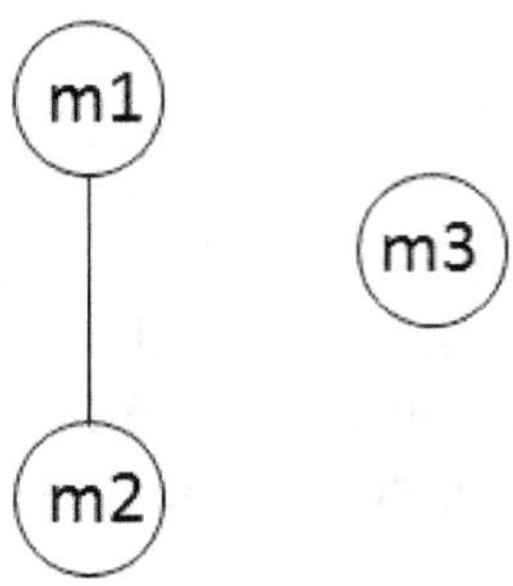

Figure 1.2. DMMC graph of the class given in Figure 1.1

Example 1.2
Figure 1.3 shows the IMAC graph that models the Java code given in Figure 1.1. The graph is similar to the one given in Figure 1.2 with an additional edge to represent the invocation of *m2* by *m3*.

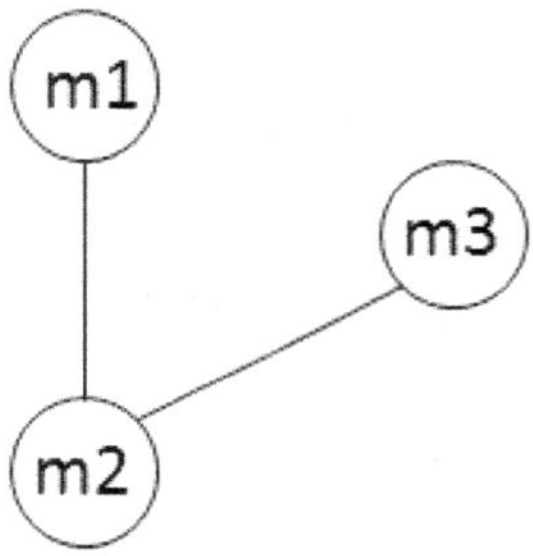

Figure 1.3. IMAC graph of the class given in Figure 1.1

1.1.3. Method-Attribute Connectivity Graph

Method-Attribute Connectivity (MAC) graph is an undirected graph that consists of nodes and undirected edges. A circular node represents an attribute and a rectangle node represents a method. The reference (i.e., definition or use) of an attribute by a method is represented by an edge connecting the nodes that represent the attribute and the method. This edge indicates a direct cohesive interaction between the attribute and method.

Example 1.3
Figure 1.4 shows the MAC graph that models the Java code given in Figure 1.1. The graph has two circular nodes and three rectangle nodes. The graph shows that method m1 references attribute a1, and method m2 references attributes a1 and a2. Method m3 does not reference any attribute.

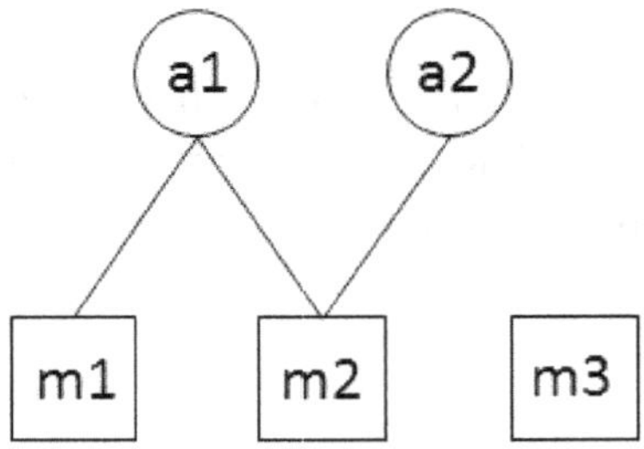

Figure 1.4. MAC graph of the class given in Figure 1.1

1.2. Matrix-Based Class Models

1.2.1. Direct Method-Attribute Matrix

The Direct Method-Attribute (DMA) matrix is a binary $k \times l$ matrix, where k is the number of methods and l is the number of attributes in the class of interest. The DMA matrix has rows indexed by the methods and columns indexed by the attributes, and so for $1 \leq i \leq k$, $1 \leq j \leq l$,

$$m_{ij} = \begin{cases} 1 & \text{if } i\text{th method directly references } j\text{th attribute,} \\ 0 & \text{otherwise} \end{cases}$$

A binary value of 1 in the DMA matrix at row i and column j indicates a direct cohesive interaction between method i and attribute j.

Example 1.4

The Java code given in Figure 1.5 shows an example class that has five methods and three attributes. Figure 1.6 shows the DMA matrix of the class. The matrix shows that m1 references *a1*, *m2* references *a2*, and *m3* and *m4* reference *a3*.

1.2.2. Indirect Method-Attribute Matrix

The Indirect Method-Attribute (IMA) matrix is a binary $k \times l$ matrix, where k is the number of methods and l is the number of attributes in the class of interest. The IMA matrix has rows indexed by the methods and columns indexed by the attributes, and so for $1 \leq i \leq k$, $1 \leq j \leq l$,

$$m_{ij} = \begin{cases} 1 & \text{if } i\text{th method directly or transitively references } j\text{th attribute,} \\ 0 & \text{otherwise} \end{cases}$$

An attribute is transitively referenced by method m_j if the attribute is directly referenced by method m_i and method m_j directly or transitively invokes method m_j. A binary value of 1 in the IMA matrix at row i and column j indicates a direct or indirect cohesive interaction between method i and attribute j.

```
public class Example_2{
        private int a1,a2,a3;
        public void m1(int x){
                if (x==0) System.out.println("a1 is not initialized");
                else System.out.println(a1=x);
        }
        public void m2(int x){
                if (x==0) System.out.println("a2 is not initialized");
                else System.out.println(a2=x);
        }
        public void m3(int x,int y){
                m1(x);
                if (y==0) System.out.println("a3 is not initialized");
                else System.out.println(a3=x);
        }
        public void m4(int x,int y){
                m2(x);
                if (y==0) System.out.println("a3 is not initialized");
                else System.out.println(a3=x);
        }
        public void m5(int x,int y,int z){
                m4(x,y);
                m2(z);
        }
}
```

Figure 1.5. Java class Example_2

Example 1.5

Figure 1.7 shows the IMA matrix of the class given in Figure 1.5. The matrix shows that methods *m1* and *m2* directly reference attributes *a1* and *a2*, respectively, and methods *m3* and *m4* directly reference attribute *a3*. In addition, the matrix shows five binary values of 1, highlighted in boldface for clarification purposes, to represent the transitive references of attribute *a1* by methods *m3* and *m5*, attribute *a2* by methods *m4* and *m5*, and attributes *a3* by method *m5*.

	a1	a2	a3
m1	1	0	0
m2	0	1	0
m3	0	0	1
m4	0	0	1
m5	0	0	0

Figure 1.6. The DMA matrix for the *Example_2* class

	a1	a2	a3
m1	1	0	0
m2	0	1	0
m3	**1**	0	1
m4	0	**1**	1
m5	**1**	**1**	**1**

Figure 1.7. The IMA matrix for the *Example_2* class

1.2.3. Direct Method Invocation Matrix

The Direct Method Invocation (DMI) matrix is a square binary *k*×*k* matrix, where k is the number of methods in the class of interest. The DMI matrix has rows and columns indexed by the methods, and so for $1 \leq I \leq k$, $1 \leq j \leq k$,

$$m_{ij} = \begin{cases} 1 & \text{if } i\text{th method directly invokes the } j\text{th method,} \\ 0 & \text{otherwise} \end{cases}$$

A binary value of 1 in the DMI matrix at row *i* and column *j* indicates a cohesive direct method invocation interaction between methods *i* and *j*.

Example 1.6

The Java code given in Figure 1.8 shows an example class that has four methods and four attributes. Figure 1.9 shows the DMI matrix of the class. The matrix shows that the *showInfo* method invokes directly the *showExtraInfo* method and the *showExtraInfo* method invokes directly the *showAddress* method.

```
class AccountDialog {
        String holderName;
        int accountNumber;
        Date startingDate;
        Address holderAddress;
        void ShowInfo(String a, int a, Date d, Card c){
                ShowExtraInfo();
        }
        void ShowAddress(Address a){
        }
        void ShowExtraInfo(){
                ShowAddress(Address s=new Address());
        }
        String readName(){
        }
}
```

Figure 1.8. Java class *AccountDialog*

	show Info	showA ddress	showExt raInfo	readNa me
showInfo	0	0	1	0
showAddress	0	0	0	0
showExtraInfo	0	1	0	0
readName	0	0	0	0

Figure 1.9. The DMI matrix for the *AccountDialog* class given in Figure 1.8

2.2.4. Indirect Method Invocation Matrix

The Indirect Method Invocation (IMI) matrix is a square binary $k \times k$ matrix, where k is the number of methods in the class of interest. The DMI matrix has rows and columns indexed by the methods, and so for $1 \leq I \leq k$, $1 \leq j \leq k$,

$$m_{ij} = \begin{cases} 1 & \text{if } i\text{th method directly or transitively invokes the } j\text{th method,} \\ 0 & \text{otherwise} \end{cases}$$

A method m_i transitively invokes method m_j if method m_i directly invokes method m_k which directly or transitively invokes method m_j. A binary value of 1 in the IMI matrix at row i and column j indicates a cohesive direct or transitive method invocation interaction between methods i and j.

Example 1.7

Figure 1.10 shows the IMI matrix of the class given in Figure 1.8. The matrix shows that the *showInfo* method invokes directly or transitively each of the *showAddress* and the *showExtraInfo* methods, and the *showExtraInfo* method invokes directly or transitively the *showAddress* method.

	show Info	showA ddress	showExt raInfo	readNa me
showInfo	0	1	1	0
showAddress	0	0	0	0
showExtraInfo	0	1	0	0
readName	0	0	0	0

Figure 1.10. The IMI matrix for the *AccountDialog* class given in Figure 1.8

1.2.5. Direct Attribute-Type Matrix

The Direct Attribute-Type (DAT) matrix is a binary $k \times l$ matrix, where k is the number of methods and l is the number of distinct attribute types in the class of interest. The DAT matrix has rows indexed by the methods and columns indexed by the distinct attribute types, and so for $1 \leq i \leq k$, $1 \leq j \leq l$,

$$m_{ij} = \begin{cases} 1 & \text{if the } j\text{th attribute type is a type of at least one of the} \\ & \text{paramters or return of the } i\text{th method,} \\ 0 & \text{otherwise} \end{cases}$$

A binary value of 1 in the DAT matrix indicates a cohesive attribute-method interaction. A cohesive method-method interaction is represented in the DAT matrix by two rows that share binary values of 1 in a column. Similarly, a cohesive attribute-attribute interaction is represented in the DAT matrix by two columns sharing binary values of 1 in a row.

Example 1.8

Figure 1.11 shows the DAT matrix of the *AccountDialog* class given in Figure 1.8. The matrix shows that three of the attribute types are used by the *showInfo* method, one of the attribute types is used by the *showAddress* method, and one of the attributes is used by the *readName* method (as a return type). In addition, the matrix shows that the *showInfo* and *readName* methods share an attribute type, and the *String* attribute type is shared between two methods. The DAT matrix does not include the parameter type Card because it does not match any of the attribute types.

	String	int	Date	Address
showInfo	1	1	1	0
showAddress	0	0	0	1
showExtraInfo	0	0	0	0
readName	1	0	0	0

Figure 1.11. The DAT matrix for the *AccountDialog* class given in Figure 1.8

1.2.6. Indirect Attribute-Type Matrix

The Indirect Attribute-Type (IAT) matrix is a binary $k \times l$ matrix, where k is the number of methods and l is the number of distinct attribute types in the class of interest. The IAT matrix has rows indexed by the methods and columns indexed by the distinct attribute types, and so for $1 \leq i \leq k$, $1 \leq j \leq l$,

$$m_{ij} = \begin{cases} 1 & \text{if the } j\text{th attribute type is a type of at least one of the} \\ & \text{paramters or return of the } i\text{th method or a method} \\ & \text{directly or transitively invoked by method } i, \\ 0 & \text{otherwise} \end{cases}$$

A binary value of 1 in the IAT matrix indicates a cohesive direct or transitive attribute-method interaction. It indicates that the attribute type matches the parameter type of the method or the methods directly or transitively invoked by the method. The IAT matrix can be generated from both DAT and IMI matrices by applying the algorithm given in Figure 1.12. The algorithm modifies the DAT matrix by replacing the row of the caller by the result of applying the logic OR for each corresponding cell in the rows representing the call originator and call recipient.

```
Algorithm: Constructing IAT matrix
Input: DAT and IMI matrices
Output: IAT matrix
Steps:
for i=1 to no. of rows in DAT matrix
        for j=1 to no. of columns in DAT matrix
                IAT[i,j]=DAT[i,j]
for i=1 to no. of rows in IMI matrix
        for j=1 to no. of columns in IMI matrix
                if (i≠j AND IMI[i,j]=1) then
                        for k=1 to no. of columns in DAT matrix
                                IAT[i,k]=DAT[i,k] OR DAT[j,k]
```

Figure 1.12. Algorithm for constructing the IAT matrix

Example 1.9

Figure 1.13 shows the IAT matrix of the *AccountDialog* class given in Figure 1.8. The matrix is similar to the DAT matrix given in Figure 1.11 except that the *showInfo* and *showExtraInfo* methods use the *Address* attribute type transitively.

	String	int	Date	Address
showInfo	1	1	1	1
showAddress	0	0	0	1
showExtraInfo	0	0	0	1
readName	1	0	0	0

Figure 1.13. The IAT matrix for the *AccountDialog* class given in Figure 1.8

2.2.7. Direct Parameter-Type Matrix

The Direct Parameter-Type (DPT) matrix is a binary $k \times l$ matrix, where k is the number of methods and l is the number of distinct parameter types in the class of interest. The DPT matrix has rows indexed by the methods and columns indexed by the distinct parameter types, and so for $1 \leq i \leq k$, $1 \leq j \leq l$,

$$m_{ij} = \begin{cases} 1 & \text{if the } j\text{th type is a type of at least one of the} \\ & \text{paramtersof the } i\text{th method,} \\ 0 & \text{otherwise} \end{cases}$$

A cohesive method-method interaction is represented in the DPT matrix by two rows that share binary values of 1 in a column.

Example 1.10

Figure 1.14 shows the DPT matrix of the *AccountDialog* class given in Figure 1.8. The matrix shows that four of the parameter types are used by the *showInfo* method, one of the parameter types is used by the *showAddress* method, and none of the parameter types is used by any of the *readName* and *showExtraInfo* methods. The matrix shows that none of the method pairs share a parameter type.

1.2.8. Indirect Parameter-Type Matrix

The Indirect Parameter-Type (IPT) matrix is a binary $k \times l$ matrix, where k is the number of methods and l is the number of distinct parameter types in the class of interest. The IPT matrix has rows indexed by the methods and columns indexed by the distinct parameter types, and so for $1 \leq i \leq k$, $1 \leq j \leq l$,

$$m_{ij} = \begin{cases} 1 & \text{if the } j\text{th type is a type of at least one of the} \\ & \text{paramtersof the } i\text{th method or a method directly} \\ & \text{or transitively invoked by method } i, \\ 0 & \text{otherwise} \end{cases}$$

A cohesive method-method interaction is represented in the IPT matrix by two rows that share binary values of 1 in a column.

	String	int	Date	Address	Card
showInfo	1	1	1	0	1
showAddress	0	0	0	1	0
showExtraInfo	0	0	0	0	0
readName	0	0	0	0	0

Figure 1.14. The DPT matrix for the *AccountDialog* class given in Figure 1.8

Example 1.11

Figure 1.15 shows the IPT matrix of the *AccountDialog* class given in Figure 1.8. The matrix shows that the five considered parameter types are directly or transitively used by the *showInfo* method, one of the parameter types is directly or transitively used by each of the *showAddress* and *showExtraInfo* methods, and none of the parameter types is directly or transitively used by the *readName* method. The matrix shows that three pairs of methods share a parameter type.

	String	int	Date	Address	Card
showInfo	1	1	1	1	1
showAddress	0	0	0	1	0
showExtraInfo	0	0	0	1	0
readName	0	0	0	0	0

Figure 1.15. The IPT matrix for the *AccountDialog* class given in Figure 1.8

Summary

This chapter provided definitions and descriptions for the key models used to represent the class members and their interactions. Existing class cohesion measures use two main types of class models: graph-based and matrix-based. Each of these types of models can represent direct and indirect interactions. They can also model method-method interactions caused by direct or transitive method invocations and method-attribute interactions caused by direct or transitive attribute references. Some matrix-based models consider the interactions between methods and attribute types or method parameter types.

CHAPTER 2 COHESION MEASURES

Several measures have been proposed in the literature to quantify the degree of cohesion in object-oriented systems at different abstraction levels, including method measures and class measures. The class cohesion measures can be classified according to different perspectives, such as the types of interactions considered, the development phase during which they are applicable, and the measurement approach they follow. In this chapter, we consider twenty measures, including $LCOM_{CK1}$, $LCOM_{CK2}$, $LCOM_L$, $LCOM_{HM}$, $LCOM_H$, Coh, TCC, LCC, DC_D, DC_I, CC, SCOM, LSCC, CAMC, NHD, MMAC, CBMC, ICBMC, OL_n, and PCCC.

These measures are classified according to the approach they follow to measure cohesion. Three main approaches are identified including (1) use of attributes or types, (2) share of attributes or types, and (3) measuring graph connectivity. The measures can be classified according to the development phase during which they are applicable. High-level design (HLD) cohesion measures identify potential cohesion issues early in the HLD phase. During the HLD phase, the interactions between the methods and attributes in a class are not precisely known or defined. Low-level design (LLD) cohesion measures use finer-grained information than that used by the HLD cohesion measures. In these measures, the referencing of an attribute by a method is considered to be an interaction. Among measures considered in this chapter, only CAMC, NHD, and MMAC are applicable during the high-level design phase, whereas the rest are applicable during the low-level design phase.

2.1. Use of Attribute/Type Measures

The description of three measures is provided here. These measures are based on simply counting the total number of referenced attributes or parameter types considered by the methods in the class of interest, regardless of the allocation of these references.

2.1.1. Coh

Coh is an LLD-based measure introduced by Briand et al. (1998). The measure uses the DMA matrix (Section 1.2.1), and it is based on counting the number of distinct attributes referenced by each method. The measure is formally defined as follows.

$$Coh = \frac{\sum_{i=1}^{l}\sum_{j=1}^{k} m_{ij}}{l \times k},$$

where l is the number of attributes and k is the number methods. The definition of m_{ij} is provided in Section 1.2.1.

Example 2.1
Given the DMA matrix shown in Figure 1.6, the value of Coh is computed as follows:

$$Coh = \frac{4}{3 \times 5} = 0.267$$

2.1.2. LCOM$_H$

Lack of Cohesion in Methods (LCOM$_H$) is an LLD-based measure introduced by Henderson-Sellers (1996) to indicate the degree of absence of cohesion in a class of interest. The measure uses the DMA matrix (Section 1.2.1), and it is based on counting the number of distinct attributes referenced by each method. The measure is formally defined as follows.

$$LCOM_H = \frac{l \times k - \sum_{i=1}^{l} \sum_{j=1}^{k} m_{ij}}{l \times k - l},$$

where l is the number of attributes and k is the number methods. The definition of m_{ij} is provided in Section 1.2.1.

Example 2.2
Given the DMA matrix shown in Figure 1.6, the value of $LCOM_H$ is computed as follows:

$$LCOM_H = \frac{3 \times 5 - 4}{3 \times 5 - 3} = 0.917$$

2.1.3. CAMC

Cohesion Among Methods in a Class (CAMC) is an HLD-based measure introduced by Henderson-Sellers (1996). The measure uses the DPT matrix (Section 1.2.7), and it is based on counting the number of distinct parameter types of each method. CAMC is based on assumption that the types of the method parameters are expected to match the types of the attributes accessed by the method. The measure is formally defined as follows.

$$CAMC = \frac{\sum_{i=1}^{l} \sum_{j=1}^{k} m_{ij}}{l \times k},$$

where l is the number of distinct parameter types and k is the number methods. The definition of m_{ij} is provided in Section 1.2.7.

Example 2.3
Given the DPT matrix shown in Figure 1.14, the value of CAMC is computed as follows:

$$CAMC = \frac{5}{5 \times 4} = 0.25$$

2.2. Share of Attribute/Type Measures

This section provides descriptions for eleven measures. Each of these measures considers two methods in the class of interest to be cohesively related if they share attributes or share types of attributes or parameters. In some of these measures, a pair of methods is considered to fully interact if they share at least one common attribute or type of attribute or parameter (i.e., a common attribute or type of attribute or parameter is referenced by each of the two methods). Other measures use the number of shared attributes types of attributes or parameters as a basis to measure the degree of interaction between each pair of methods. This is referred to as *similarity degree.*

2.2.1. $LCOM_{CK1}$

$LCOM_{CK1}$ is an LLD-based measure introduced by Chidamber and Kemerer (1991). The measure uses the DMMC graph (Section 1.1.1) or DMA matrix (Section 1.2.1), and it measures the absence of cohesion. The measure is defined as the number of method pairs that do not share attributes. Using the DMMC graph, $LCOM_{CK1}$ is formally defined as follows.

$$LCOM_{CK1} = \frac{n \times (n-1)}{2} - e\,,$$

where n and e are the number of nodes and edges, respectively, in DMMC. Using the DMA matrix, $LCOM_{CK1}$ is formally defined as follows.

$$LCOM_{CK1} = \frac{k \times (k-1)}{2} - \sum_{i=1}^{k-1} \sum_{j=i+1}^{k} \bigvee_{p=1}^{l} (m_{ip} \vee m_{jp})\,,$$

where l is the number of attributes and k is the number methods. The definition of m_{ij} is provided in Section 1.2.1.

Example 2.4

The DMMC graph given in Figure 1.2 has three nodes and one edge, and therefore, the value of $LCOM_{CK1}$ is computed as follows.

$$LCOM_{CK1} = \frac{3 \times (3-1)}{2} - 1 = 2$$

Example 2.5
The DMA given in Figure 1.6 shows that the class has five methods, which means that there is a total of ten method pairs. Only one method pair, which is (m3, m4) shares a common attribute and the none of the rest nine method pairs shares an attribute. Therefore, the value of $LCOM_{CK1}$ is computed as follows.

$$LCOM_{CK1} = \frac{5 \times (5-1)}{2} - 1 = 9$$

2.2.2. $LCOM_{CK2}$

$LCOM_{CK2}$ is an LLD-based measure introduced by Chidamber and Kemerer (1994). The measure uses the DMMC graph (Section 1.1.1) or DMA matrix (Section 1.2.1), and it measures the absence of cohesion. The measure is formally defined as follows.

$$LCOM_{CK2} = \begin{cases} P-Q & if\ P-Q \geq 0 \\ 0 & otherwise \end{cases},$$

where P is the number of pairs of methods that do not share attributes and Q is the number of pairs of methods that share attributes. Using the DMMC graph, when $P - Q \geq 0$, $LCOM_{CK2}$ is formally defined as follows.

$$LCOM_{CK2} = \frac{n \times (n-1)}{2} - 2 \times e\,,$$

where n and e are the number of nodes and edges, respectively, in DMMC. Using the DMA matrix, $LCOM_{CK2}$ is formally defined as follows.

$$LCOM_{CK2} = \frac{k \times (k-1)}{2} - 2 \times \sum_{i=1}^{k-1} \sum_{j=i+1}^{k} \bigvee_{p=1}^{l} (m_{ip} \vee m_{jp})\,,$$

where l is the number of attributes and k is the number methods. The definition of m_{ij} is provided in Section 1.2.1.

Example 2.6

The DMMC graph given in Figure 1.2 has three nodes and one edge, and therefore, the value of LCOMCK2 is computed as follows.

$$LCOM_{CK2} = \frac{3 \times (3 - 1)}{2} - 2 \times 1 = 1$$

Example 2.7

The DMA given in Figure 1.6 shows that the class has five methods, which means that there is a total of ten method pairs. Only one method pair, which is (m3, m4) shares a common attribute and none of the rest nine method pairs shares an attribute. Therefore, the value of LCOMCK2 is calculated as follows.

$$LCOM_{CK2} = \frac{5 \times (5 - 1)}{2} - 2 \times 1 = 8$$

2.2.3. TCC

Tight Class Cohesion (TCC) is an LLD-based measure introduced by Bieman and Kang (1995). The measure uses the IMA matrix (Section 1.2.2). TCC is defined as the relative number of directly connected pairs of methods, where two methods are directly connected if they are directly connected to an attribute. A method *m* is directly connected to an attribute when the attribute appears within the method's body or within the body of a method invoked by method *m* directly or transitively. In other words, using the IMA matrix, TCC is the relative number of pairs of rows that share at least a binary value "1" in a column. The measure is formally defined as follows.

$$TCC = \frac{\sum_{i=1}^{k-1} \sum_{j=i+1}^{k} \bigvee_{p=1}^{l} (m_{ip} \vee m_{jp})}{0.5 \times k \times (k - 1)},$$

where l is the number of attributes and k is the number methods. The definition of m_{ij} is provided in Section 1.2.2.

Example 2.8

The IMA matrix given in Figure 1.7 shows that the class has five methods, which means that there is a total of ten method pairs. Seven pairs share at least one attribute. These pairs are (m1, m3), (m1, m5), (m2, m4), (m2, m5), (m3, m4), (m3, m5), and (m4, m5). Therefore, the value of TCC is computed as follows.

$$TCC = \frac{7}{10} = 0.7$$

Example 2.9

Figure 2.2 shows the IMA matrix for the class given in Figure 2.1. The class has eight methods. The total number of method pairs is 8 × (8 - 1) / 2 = 28. Seven pairs share at least one attribute. These pairs are (m1, m3), (m1, m5), (m2, m4), (m2, m5), (m3, m4), (m3, m5), and (m4, m5). Therefore, the value of TCC is computed as follows.

$$TCC = \frac{7}{28} = 0.25$$

2.2.4. LCC

Loose Class Cohesion (LCC) is an LLD-based measure introduced by Bieman and Kang (1995). The measure uses the IMA matrix (Section 1.2.2). LCC is defined as the relative number of directly or transitively connected pairs of methods, where two methods are transitively connected if they are directly or indirectly connected to an attribute. A method *m*, directly connected to an attribute *j*, is indirectly connected to an attribute *i* when there is a method directly or transitively connected to both attributes *i* and *j*. Values of “1” can be added to IMA to represent the indirect connection between methods and attributes. After modifying IMA, the following formula can be applied.

$$LCC = \frac{\sum_{i=1}^{k-1}\sum_{j=i+1}^{k}\bigvee_{p=1}^{l}(m_{ip} \vee m_{jp})}{0.5 \times k \times (k-1)},$$

where *l* is the number of attributes and *k* is the number methods. The definition of m_{ij} is provided in Section 1.2.2 with the additional binary values "1" added to represent the indirect connection between methods and attributes.

```
public class Example_3{
        private int a1,a2,a3;
        public void m1(int x){
                if (x==0) System.out.println("a1 is not initialized");
                else System.out.println(a1=x);
        }
        public void m2(int x){
                if (x==0) System.out.println("a2 is not initialized");
                else System.out.println(a2=x);
        }
        public void m3(int x,int y){
                m1(x);
                if (y==0) System.out.println("a3 is not initialized");
                else System.out.println(a3=x);
        }
        public void m4(int x,int y){
                m2(x);
                if (y==0) System.out.println("a3 is not initialized");
                else System.out.println(a3=x);
        }
        public void m5(int x,int y,int z){
                m4(x,y);
                m2(z);
        }
        public void m6(){
                m8();
        }
        public void m7(){
                m8();
        }
        public void m8(){
        }
}
```

Figure 2.1. Java class Example_3

	a1	a2	a3
m1	1	0	0
m2	0	1	0
m3	1	0	1
m4	0	1	1
m5	1	1	1
m6	0	0	0
m7	0	0	0
m8	0	0	0

Figure 2.2. The IMA matrix for the *Example_3* class

Example 2.10

Figure 2.3 shows the modified version of IMA given in Figure 1.7 after adding the additional binary values "1" added to represent the indirect connection between methods and attributes. The added binary values "1" are marked in boldface. For example, method *m1*, directly connected to attribute *a1*, is indirectly connected to attribute *a2* because method *m5* is directly or transitively connected to both attributes *a1* and *a2*.

	a1	a2	a3
m1	1	**1**	**1**
m2	**1**	1	**1**
m3	1	**1**	1
m4	**1**	1	1
m5	1	1	1

Figure 2.3. The modified IMA matrix for the *Example_2* class

After generating the modified IMA, the value of LCC is computed as follows.

$$LCC = \frac{10}{0.5 \times 5 \times (5 - 1)} = 1$$

Example 2.11

Figure 2.4 shows the modified version of IMA given in Figure 2.2 after adding the additional binary values "1" added to represent the indirect connection between methods and attributes. The added binary values "1" are marked in boldface.

After generating the modified IMA, the value of LCC is computed as follows.

$$LCC = \frac{10}{0.5 \times 8 \times (8-1)} = 0.357$$

	a1	a2	a3
m1	1	**1**	**1**
m2	**1**	1	**1**
m3	1	**1**	1
m4	**1**	1	1
m5	1	1	1
m6	0	0	0
m7	0	0	0
m8	0	0	0

Figure 2.4. The modified IMA matrix for the *Example_3* class

2.2.5. DC$_D$

Degree of Cohesion-Direct (DC$_D$) is an LLD-based measure introduced by Badri and Badri (2004). The measure uses the IMA matrix (Section 1.2.2). DC$_D$ is defined as the relative number of directly connected pairs of methods, where two methods are directly connected if they satisfy the condition mentioned for TCC or if the two methods directly or transitively invoke the same method. The measure is formally defined as follows.

$$DC_D = \frac{\left(\sum_{i=1}^{k-1}\sum_{j=i+1}^{k}\bigvee_{p=1}^{l}(m_{ip} \vee m_{jp})\right) + d}{0.5 \times k \times (k-1)},$$

where l is the number of attributes, k is the number methods, and d is the number of pairs of methods that directly or transitively invoke the same method if the pairs of methods are not already counted within the directly connected pairs of methods. The definition of m_{ij} is provided in Section 1.2.2.

Example 2.12
The class given in Figure 2.1 shows that both methods m6 and m7 invoke method m8, and therefore, methods m6 and m7 are connected and this connection is not already considered when computing TCC. Given this fact and the IMA matrix given in Figure 2.2, the value of DC_D is computed as follows.

$$DC_D = \frac{7+1}{28} = 0.286$$

2.2.6. DC_I

Degree of Cohesion-Indirect (DC_I) is an LLD-based measure introduced by Badri and Badri (2004). The measure uses the modified IMA matrix (Section 2.2.4). DC_D is defined as the relative number of directly or transitively connected pairs of methods, where two methods are transitively connected if they satisfy the same condition mentioned for LCC or if the two methods directly or transitively invoke the same method. The measure is formally defined as follows.

$$DC_I = \frac{\left(\sum_{i=1}^{k-1} \sum_{j=i+1}^{k} \bigvee_{p=1}^{l} (m_{ip} \vee m_{jp})\right) + d}{0.5 \times k \times (k-1)},$$

where l is the number of attributes, k is the number methods, and d is the number of pairs of methods that directly or transitively invoke the same method if the pairs of methods are not already counted within the directly or transitively connected pairs of methods. The definition of m_{ij} is provided in Section 1.2.2 with the additional binary values "1" added to represent the indirect connection between methods and attributes, as explained in Section 2.2.4.

Example 2.13
The class given in Figure 2.1 shows that both methods m6 and m7 invoke method m8, and therefore, methods m6 and m7 are connected and this connection is not already considered when computing LCC. Given this fact and the IMA matrix given in Figure 2.4, the value of DC_I is computed as follows.

$$DC_I = \frac{10 + 1}{28} = 0.393$$

2.2.7. CC

Class Cohesion (CC) is an LLD-based measure introduced by Bonja and Kidanmariam (2006). The measure uses the DMA matrix (Section 1.2.1), and it considers the similarity between each pair of methods. The measure is defined as the ratio of the summation of the similarities between all pairs of methods to the total number of pairs of methods. The similarity between methods i and j is defined as follows.

$$SC(i,j) = \frac{|I_i \cap I_j|}{|I_i \cup I_j|},$$

where I_i and I_j are the sets of attributes referenced by methods i and j, respectively. The measure is formally defined as follows.

$$CC = \frac{\sum_{i=1}^{k-1} \sum_{j=i+1}^{k} SC(i,j)}{0.5 \times k \times (k-1)},$$

where k is the number methods.

Example 2.14
Figure 2.6 shows the DMA matrix for the class given in Figure 2.5. The class has three methods and three attributes. The total number of method pairs is 3 × (3 - 1) / 2 = 3. The similarity between each pair of methods is calculated as follows.

$$SC(1,2) = \frac{1}{2} = 0.5, SC(1,3) = \frac{0}{2} = 0, and\ SC(2,3) = \frac{0}{3} = 0$$

Therefore, CC is calculated as follows.

$$CC = \frac{0.5 + 0 + 0}{0.5 \times 3 \times (3 - 1)} = 0.167$$

```
public class Example_4{
        private int a1,a2,a3;
        public void m1(int x){
                if (x==0) System.out.println("a1 is not initialized");
                else System.out.println(a1=x);
        }
        public void m2(int x){
                if (x==0)
                    System.out.println("a1 or a2 is not initialized");
                else System.out.println(a1=x+”,“+a2=x);
        }
        public void m3(int x){
                System.out.println(a3=x);
                m1(x);
                m2(x);
        }
}
```

Figure 2.5. Java class Example_4

	a1	a2	a3
m1	1	0	0
m2	1	1	0
m3	0	0	1

Figure 2.6. The DMA matrix for the *Example_4* class

2.2.8. SCOM

Sensitive Class Cohesion Metric (SCOM) is an LLD-based measure introduced by Fernandez and Pena (2006). The measure uses the DMA matrix (Section 1.2.1), and it considers the similarity between each pair of methods. The measure is defined as the ratio of the summation of the similarities between all pairs of methods to the total number of pairs of methods. The similarity between methods *i* and *j* is defined as follows.

$$SS(i,j) = \frac{|I_i \cap I_j| \times |I_i \cup I_j|}{\min(|I_i|, |I_j|) \times l},$$

where I_i and I_j are the sets of attributes referenced by methods *i* and *j*, respectively, and *l* is the number of attributes. The measure is formally defined as follows.

$$SCOM = \frac{\sum_{i=1}^{k-1} \sum_{j=i+1}^{k} SS(i,j)}{0.5 \times k \times (k-1)},$$

where *k* is the number methods.

Example 2.15

Given the DMA matrix shown in Figure 2.6, The similarity between each pair of methods is calculated as follows.

$$SS(1,2) = \frac{1 \times 2}{1 \times 3} = 0.667, SS(1,3) = \frac{0 \times 2}{1 \times 3} = 0, and\ SS(2,3) = \frac{0 \times 3}{1 \times 3} = 0$$

Therefore, SCOM is calculated as follows.

$$SCOM = \frac{0.667 + 0 + 0}{0.5 \times 3 \times (3-1)} = 0.222$$

2.2.9. LSCC

Low-level design Similarity-based Class Cohesion (LSCC) is an LLD-based measure introduced by Al Dallal and Briand (2012). The measure uses the IMA matrix (Section 1.2.2), and it considers the similarity between each pair of methods. The measure is defined as the ratio of the summation of the similarities between all pairs of methods to the total number of pairs of methods. The similarity between methods *i* and *j* is defined as follows.

$$SL(i,j) = \frac{|I_i \cap I_j|}{l},$$

where I_i and I_j are the sets of attributes referenced by methods i and j, respectively, and l is the number of attributes. The measure is formally defined as follows.

$$LSCC = \begin{cases} 0 & if\ l = 0\ and\ k > 1 \\ 1 & if\ (l > 0\ and\ k = 0) or\ k = 1 \\ \frac{\sum_{i=1}^{k-1}\sum_{j=i+1}^{k} SL(i,j)}{0.5 \times k \times (k-1)} & otherwise \end{cases},$$

where k is the number methods and l is the number of attributes. Alternatively, the measure can be calculated using the following formula.

$$LSCC = \begin{cases} 0 & if\ l = 0\ and\ k > 1 \\ 1 & if\ (l > 0\ and\ k = 0) or\ k = 1 \\ \frac{\sum_{i=1}^{l} x_i \times (x_i - 1)}{l \times k \times (k-1)} & otherwise \end{cases},$$

where x_i is the number of 1s in the ith column of the IMA matrix

Example 2.16

Figure 2.7 shows the IMA matrix of the class given in Figure 2.5. The similarity between each pair of methods is calculated as follows.

$$SL(1,2) = \frac{1}{3} = 0.333, SL(1,3) = \frac{1}{3} = 0.333, and\ SL(2,3) = \frac{2}{3} = 0.667$$

Therefore, LSCC is calculated as follows.

$$LSCC = \frac{0.333 + 0.333 + 0.667}{0.5 \times 3 \times (3-1)} = 0.444$$

Alternatively, LSCC can be calculated as follows.

$$LSCC = \frac{3 \times (3-1) + 2 \times (2-1) + 1 \times (1-1)}{3 \times 3 \times (3-1)} = 0.444$$

	a1	a2	a3
m1	1	0	0
m2	1	1	0
m3	1	1	1

Figure 2.7. The IMA matrix for the *Example_4* class

2.2.10. NHD

Normalized Hamming Distance (NHD) is an HLD-based measure introduced by Counsell et al. (2006). The measure uses the DPT matrix (Section 1.2.7), and it considers the average parameter agreement between each pair of methods. The parameter agreement between a pair of methods is defined as the number of entries in which the corresponding rows in the DPT matrix match. The measure is formally defined as follows.

$$NHD = \frac{\sum_{i=1}^{k-1}\sum_{j=i+1}^{k}\sum_{p=1}^{l}\overline{(m_{ip} \oplus m_{jp})}}{0.5 \times l \times k \times (k-1)},$$

where l is the number of distinct parameter types and k is the number methods. The definition of m_{ij} is provided in Section 1.2.7. Alternatively, the measure can be calculated using the following formula.

$$NHD = 1 - \frac{\sum_{i=1}^{l} x_i \times (k - x_i)}{0.5 \times l \times k \times (k-1)}$$

where x_i is the number of 1s in the jth column of the DPT matrix.

Example 2.17
Given the DPT matrix shown in Figure 1.14, the value of NHD is computed as follows:

$$NHD = \frac{0+1+1+4+4+5}{0.5 \times 5 \times 4 \times (4-1)} = 0.5$$

Alternatively, NHD can be calculated as follows.

$$NHD = 1 - \frac{1 \times (4-1) + 1 \times (4-1) + 1 \times (4-1) + 1 \times (4-1) + 1 \times (4-1)}{0.5 \times 5 \times 4 \times (4-1)} = 0.5$$

2.2.11. MMAC

Method-Method through Attributes Cohesion (MMAC) is an HLD-based measure introduced by Al Dallal and Briand (2010). The measure uses the IAT matrix (Section 1.2.6), and it considers the average similarity between each pair of methods. The measure is defined as the ratio of the summation of the similarities between all pairs of methods to the total number of pairs of methods. The similarity between methods i and j is defined as follows.

$$SM(i,j) = \frac{|I_i \cap I_j|}{l},$$

where I_i and I_j are the sets of attribute types that match parameters or return types of methods i and j, respectively, and l is the number of attribute types. The measure is formally defined as follows.

$$MMAC = \begin{cases} 0 & if\ l = 0\ or\ k = 0 \\ 1 & if\ k = 1 \\ \frac{\sum_{i=1}^{k-1} \sum_{j=i+1}^{k} SM(i,j)}{0.5 \times k \times (k-1)} & otherwise \end{cases},$$

where k is the number methods and l is the number of distinct attribute types. Alternatively, the measure can be calculated using the following formula.

$$MMAC = \begin{cases} 0 & if\ l = 0\ or\ k = 0 \\ 1 & if\ k = 1 \\ \frac{\sum_{i=1}^{l} x_i \times (x_i - 1)}{l \times k \times (k-1)} & otherwise \end{cases},$$

where x_i is the number of 1s in the ith column of the IAT matrix.

Example 2.18

Given the IAT matrix shown in Figure 1.13. The similarity between each pair of methods is calculated as follows.

$$SM(1,2) = \frac{1}{4} = 0.25, SM(1,3) = \frac{1}{4} = 0.25, SM(1,4) = \frac{1}{4} = 0.25,$$

$$SM(2,3) = \frac{1}{4} = 0.25, SM(2,4) = \frac{0}{4} = 0, and\ SM(3,4) = \frac{0}{4} = 0$$

Therefore, MMAC is calculated as follows.

$$MMAC = \frac{0.25 + 0.25 + 0.25 + 0.25 + 0 + 0}{0.5 \times 4 \times (4 - 1)} = 0.167$$

Alternatively, MMAC can be calculated as follows.

$$MMAC = \frac{2 \times (2 - 1) + 1 \times (1 - 1) + 1 \times (1 - 1) + 3 \times (3 - 1)}{4 \times 4 \times (4 - 1)} = 0.167$$

2.3. Graph-Connectivity Measures

In a graph-based class model, the pattern that results from the way in which the nodes that represent attributes and methods are connected by edges is referred to as the connectivity pattern. Intuitively, a class with a more complex connectivity pattern is more cohesive than a class with a less complex connectivity pattern (Xu and Zhou 2001). Connectivity-based measures view cohesion as the degree of connectivity between all of the members of a class, and, therefore, from this perspective, they more comprehensively indicate cohesion than measures that are based on other measuring approaches. Connectivity-based measures have several advantages over measures that use other measuring approaches. First, connectivity measures directly or indirectly address whether the reference graph of the class is connected or disjointed. A class with a disjoint reference graph is given a low cohesion value because such a class can be easily divided into two or more classes. Second, even when the graph is connected, some connectivity measures precisely predict the degree of connectivity of the class members, which indicates the complexity of the connectivity pattern of the class reference graph. Therefore, cohesion conclusions that are drawn by applying such measures are more consistent with intuition than those that are drawn by applying other measures (Xu and Zhou 2001). This section provides descriptions for six graph-connectivity class cohesion measures. All these measures are LLD-based measures.

2.3.1. $LCOM_L$

Lack of Cohesion in Methods ($LCOM_L$) is an LLD-based measure introduced by Li and Henry (1993) to indicate the degree of absence of cohesion in a class of interest. The measure uses the DMMC graph (Section 1.1.1), and it is defined as the number of connected components in the DMMC graph.

Example 2.19
The DMMC graph given in Figure 1.2 has two disjoint components; one includes the nodes representing methods m1 and m2, and the other includes the node representing method m3. Therefore, the value of $LCOM_L$ is 2.

2.3.2. $LCOM_{HM}$

Lack of Cohesion in Methods ($LCOM_{HM}$) is an LLD-based measure introduced by Hitz and Montazeri (1995) to indicate the degree of absence of cohesion in a class of interest. The measure uses the IMMC graph (Section 1.1.2), and it is defined as the number of connected components in the IMMC graph. To differentiate between classes that have $LCOM_{HM}$ value of “1”, the following connectivity measure is applied.

$$connectivity = 2 \times \frac{e - (n-1)}{(n-1) \times (n-2)},$$

where n and e are the number of nodes and edges in the IMMC graph, respectively.

Example 2.20

The IMMC graph given in Figure 1.3 has one component including the nodes that represent methods m1, m2, and m3. Therefore, the value of $LCOM_{HM}$ is 1. The number of nodes and edges in the graph are 3 and 2, respectively. Therefore, the value of connectivity is calculated as follows.

$$connectivity = 2 \times \frac{2 - (3 - 1)}{(3 - 1) \times (3 - 2)} = 0$$

2.3.3. CBMC

Cohesion Based on Member Connectivity (CBMC) is an LLD-based measure introduced by Chae et al. (2000). The measure uses the MAC graph (Section 1.1.3) and quantifies cohesion based on factors related to removals of sets of glue methods. The set of glue methods is the minimum set of methods by which their removal causes the graph to become disjointed. This measure defines the connectivity factor F_c of the graph that represents class *C* to be the ratio of the number of glue methods to the number of normal methods (i.e., nonspecial methods). When the nodes that represent glue methods and their connecting edges are removed from the graph, two or more connected subgraphs are formed. In this case, the original graph is considered to be the parent, whereas the resulting subgraphs are the children. Recursively, in the same manner, each child graph is decomposed into subgraphs until the subgraph has a single node that represents either a method or an attribute, or the subgraph has multiple nodes such that each node that represents a method is connected to each node that represents an attribute. In these cases, the connectivity factor of the subgraph is equal to one. The CBMC of each parent graph is calculated as the product of the connectivity factor of the parent graph and the average connectivity factors of the child graphs. Note that a graph can have several sets of glue methods. In this case, the set of glue methods that results in the highest CBMC is selected to involve in cohesion measurement. The CBMC measure is formally defined as follows.

$$CBMC(G) = F_c(G) \times F_s(G),$$

where $F_c(G) = \frac{|M(G)|}{|N(G)|}$, $M(G)$ is the number of glue methods in graph G, $N(G)$ is the number of non-special methods in graph G, $F_s(G) = \frac{\sum_{i=1}^{n} CBMC(G^i)}{n}$, n is the number of child nodes of G, and glue methods is the minimum set of methods for which their removal causes the MAC graph to become disjointed.

Example 2.21

The Java code given in Figure 2.8 shows an example class that has three methods and three attributes. The graph G_c, which is depicted in Figure 2.9, is the MAC graph for class Example_5 given in Figure 2.8. The graph has three nodes representing attributes, three nodes representing methods, and six edges representing the reference of the attributes by the methods. There is only one set of glue methods graph G_c, and it includes m_1, which means that $F_c = \frac{1}{3}$. Graphs G_{c1} and G_{c2} result from removing the node that represents the glue method and the two interactions that are connected to it. These graphs are not further decomposed because G_{c1} includes a single node and G_{c2} has two methods, wherein each of them is linked with each attribute. As a result, the average F for the child graphs is one, and, therefore, CBMC is calculated as follows.

$$CBMC(G_c) = \frac{1}{3} \times \frac{1+1}{2} = \frac{1}{3}$$

2.3.4. ICBMC

Improved Cohesion Based on Member Connectivity (ICBMC) is an LLD-based measure introduced by Xu and Zhou (2001, 2003). The measure uses the MAC graph (Section 1.1.3) and quantifies cohesion based on factors related to removals of sets of cut sets. A cut set is the minimum set of edges such that their removal causes the graph to become disjointed. This measure defines the connectivity factor as the ratio of the number of edges in a cut set to the product of the number of attributes and the number of nonspecial methods. When removing edges in a cut set, the parent graph is again split into two child graphs.

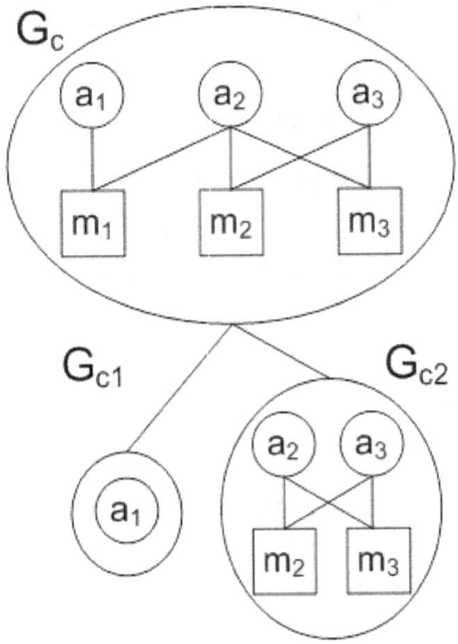

Figure 2.9. Application of CBMC to class *Example_5* given in Figure 2.8.

Recursively, in the same manner, each child graph is decomposed into two graphs until the graph has either a single node that represents a method or a single node that represents an attribute; either has one or more edges. Such a graph is called an elementary graph. The connectivity factor of an elementary graph equals one. ICBMC of each parent graph is similarly calculated in the manner in which CBMC is calculated. Note that a graph can have several cut sets. In this case, the cut set that results in the highest ICBMC is selected to involve in cohesion calculation. The CBMC measure is formally defined as follows.

$$ICBMC(G) = F_c(G) \times F_s(G)\,,$$

where $F_c(G) = \frac{|M(G)|}{|N(G)|}$, $M(G)$ is the number of edges in the cut set of G, $N(G)$ is the number of non-special methods in graph G multiplied by the number of attributes, $F_s(G) = \frac{\sum_{i=1}^{2} ICBMC(G^i)}{2}$, and cut set is the minimum set of edges such that their removal causes the MAC graph to become disjointed.

```
class Example_5 {
        int a1;
        int a2;
        int a3;
        void m1(){
                a1=a2;
        }
        void m2(){
                a2=a3;
        }
        void m3(){
                a3=a2;
        }
}
```

Figure 2.8. Java class *Example_5*

Example 2.22

The graph G_c, given in Figure 2.10, is the MAC graph for class Example_5 given in Figure 2.8. There is only one possible cut set for this graph, and it includes the edge that connects m_1 to a_2, which means that $F_c(G_c) = \frac{1}{3\times 3} = \frac{1}{9}$. Graphs G_{c1} and G_{c2} result from removing the edge that is included in the cut set. G_{c1} is an elementary graph, whereas G_{c2} is not. G_{c2} is decomposed into two elementary graphs by removing two edges that are included in a cut set. The connectivity factor of G_{c2}, $F_c(G_{c2}) = \frac{2}{2\times 2} = \frac{1}{2}$. As a result, the ICBMC for G_c is computed as follows.

$$ICBMC(G_c) = F_c(G_c) \times F_s(G_c)$$

$$= F_c(G_c) \times \frac{ICBMC(G_{c1}) + ICBMC(G_{c2})}{2}$$

$$= F_c(G_c) \times \frac{1 + F_c(G_{c2}) \times F_s(G_{c2})}{2}$$

$$= F_c(G_c) \times \frac{1 + F_c(G_{c2}) \times \frac{ICBMC(G_{c1.1}) + ICBMC(G_{c2.2})}{2}}{2}$$

$$= \frac{1}{9} \times \frac{1 + \frac{1}{2} \times \frac{1+1}{2}}{2} = 0.083$$

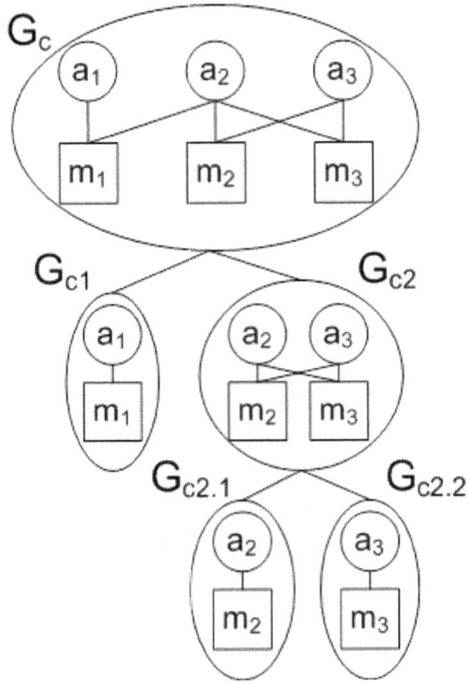

Figure 2.10. Application of ICBMC to class *Example_5* given in Figure 2.8.

2.3.5. OLn

Yang (Yang 2002) has proposed an iteratively calculated LLD-based class cohesion measure, OL_n, wherein n refers to the number of iterations that are used to calculate OL. The measure uses the MAC graph (Section 1.1.3). In each iteration, the strength S_a of each attribute a and the strength S_m of each method m are calculated. Initially, the strength of each method is set to a value of one. S_a is calculated as the ratio of the summation of the strengths of the methods that are directly connected to attribute *a* to the total number of normal methods in the class. Similarly, S_m is calculated as the ratio of the summation of the strengths of the attributes that are directly connected to method *m* and the total number of attributes in the class. The class cohesion that is calculated in iteration *n*, OL_n, is defined as the average strengths of the attributes in the class. In each iteration, the strengths of the attributes and methods that were obtained in the previous iteration are used to calculate the updated values. This process is applied only for connected MAC graphs. If the MAC graph is disjointed, the value of OL_n is set to zero.

Example 2.23

Given the MAC graph, G_c, shown in Figure 2.9, we can calculate OL_1 as follows.

$$S_{a1} = \frac{S_{m1}}{3} = \frac{1}{3}$$

$$S_{a2} = \frac{S_{m1} + S_{m2} + S_{m3}}{3} = \frac{1+1+1}{3} = 1$$

$$S_{a3} = \frac{S_{m2} + S_{m3}}{3} = \frac{1+1}{3} = \frac{2}{3}$$

$$OL_1 = \frac{S_{a1} + S_{a2} + S_{a3}}{3} = \frac{{}^1/_3 + 1 + {}^2/_3}{3} = \frac{2}{3}$$

To compute OL_2 we proceed to the next iteration using the values obtained in the first iteration as follows.

$$S_{m1} = \frac{S_{a1} + S_{a2}}{3} = \frac{{}^1/_3 + 1}{3} = \frac{4}{9}$$

$$S_{m2} = \frac{S_{a2} + S_{a3}}{3} = \frac{1 + {}^2/_3}{3} = \frac{5}{9}$$

$$S_{m3} = \frac{S_{a2} + S_{a3}}{3} = \frac{1 + {}^2/_3}{3} = \frac{5}{9}$$

$$S_{a1} = \frac{S_{m1}}{3} = \frac{{}^4/_9}{3} = \frac{4}{27}$$

$$S_{a2} = \frac{S_{m1} + S_{m2} + S_{m3}}{3} = \frac{{}^4/_9 + {}^5/_9 + {}^5/_9}{3} = \frac{14}{27}$$

$$S_{a3} = \frac{S_{m2} + S_{m3}}{3} = \frac{{}^{5}/_{9} + {}^{5}/_{9}}{3} = \frac{10}{27}$$

$$OL_2 = \frac{S_{a1} + S_{a2} + S_{a3}}{3} = \frac{{}^{4}/_{27} + {}^{14}/_{27} + {}^{10}/_{27}}{3} = \frac{28}{81} = 0.346$$

2.3.6. PCCC

Path Connectivity Class Cohesion (PCCC) is an LLD-based measure introduced by Al Dallal (2012a) The measure uses the MAC graph (Section 1.1.3) and it is based on counting the number of simple paths in the MAC graph, where a simple path is a path in which each node occurs once at most.

In order to count the number of simple paths between a pair of nodes, an *all-simple-paths* tree has to be constructed. This tree represents all of the simple paths that originate at node *n* to every other node to which node *n* is directly or transitively connected. The procedure given in Figure 2.11 formally describes how this tree is constructed. The procedure starts by adding to the tree a node *n* for which the simple paths are to be determined. In the process, whenever a node *m* is added to the tree, the procedure traverses all of its connected edges in the reference graph. The traversed edge and another node *k*, to which the edge is connected, is added to the tree only when node *k* is not already encountered on the path from node *n* to node *m*.

Note that a graph node *m* can be represented more than once in the all-simple-paths tree of a node *n*. This means that there is more than one simple path in the graph between nodes *n* and *m*. The number of occurrences of a node *m* in the all-simple-paths tree of a node *n* represents the number of simple paths from node *n* to node *m*. As a result, the total number of simple paths from node *n* to all other nodes in the graph is equal to the number of nodes, excluding the root, in the corresponding tree.

The algorithm depicted in Figure 2.12 is used to facilitate the counting of the number of simple paths in the graph. This algorithm recursively counts the number of simple paths without constructing the required trees. Instead, it uses a *visited* array that simulates the *final* marking schema that is used in the construction process of the all-simple-paths tree.

Input: An MCA graph and a node *n* for which the simple paths are to be determined.
Output: The all-simple-paths tree for node *n*.
Procedure:

1. Add a corresponding node *n* to the tree as a root node and mark the node as *not final*.
2. *for* each tree leaf node *m* marked *not final*
    a. *for* each graph node *k* connected to the node corresponding to node *m* in the MAC graph
        i. *if* node *k* is not yet represented in the tree path from the tree root node to tree node *m*
            i.1. Add a node corresponding to node *k* as a child to tree node *m*.
            i.2. Mark the added node as *not final*.
    b. Mark tree node *m* as *final*.
3. Repeat Step 2 until all tree leaf nodes are marked *final*.

Figure 2.11. The production of an all-simple-paths tree from an MAC graph.

The maximum possible number of simple paths in an MAC graph, including the same number of nodes as in *G*, is encountered when there is an edge between each node that corresponds to a method and each node that corresponds to an attribute. This graph is called *fully connected* and referenced as an *FG*. As a result, given a set of attributes *a* and a set of methods *m* of a class *c*, the corresponding fully connected MAC graph denoted as $FG_{c,a,m}$ is formally defined as an MAC graph in which there is an edge between each node that represents an attribute in *a* and each node that represents a method in *m*. In an *FG*, the number of simple paths starting from any node that represents any attribute is the same for each attribute. This is because, in an *FG*, each node that represents an attribute is connected to the same set of nodes that represents methods; the same applies for each node that represents a method. Therefore, to count the number of simple paths in an *FG*, only two all-simple-paths trees need to be constructed: one starting from a node that represents an attribute and the other starting from a node that represents a method. Given that the number of nodes, excluding the root, in the former and latter trees are S_a and S_m, respectively, and that a and m, respectively, are the sets of considered attributes and methods in a class c, $NSP(FG_{c,a,m})$ is defined as the number of simple paths in $FG_{c,a,m}$ and is computed using the following formula.

$$NSP\left(FG_{c,a,m}\right) = |a| \times S_a + |m| \times S_m$$

```
Input: An MAC graph G
Output: Number of simple paths counter in graph G
Algorithm:
    1. counter = 0
    2. for each node n in G
          a. for each node m in G
                i. create an array visited such that each cell
                   in the array corresponds to a node in G
               ii. initialize all cells of visited to false
          b. counter = counter + traverse(G,n,visited)

function traverse(MAC graph G, node n, array visited)
    counter=0
    create an array cvisited such that each cell in the array
      corresponds to a node in G
    copy array visited to cvisited
    set the value of cvisited cell corresponding to node n to value
      true
    for each node k connected to n in G
        if the cvisited cell corresponding to node k has value false
              counter = counter + 1
              counter = counter + traverse(G,k,cvisited)
    return counter
```

Figure 2.12. Algorithm for counting the number of simple paths in an MAC graph.

The PCCC measure is defined as the ratio of the number of simple paths in MAC graph *G* to the number of simple paths in the corresponding graph *FG*. The PCCC of a class *C* with a set of attributes *a* and a set of considered methods *m*, which is represented by MAC graph *G* with $NSP(G_{c,a,m})$ simple paths, is, thus, formally defined as follows.

$$PCCC(C,a,m) = \begin{cases} 0 & if\ |a| = 0\ and\ |m| > 1, \\ 1 & if\ |a| > 0\ and\ |m| = 0, \\ \dfrac{NSP(G_{c,a,m})}{NSP(FG_{c,a,m})} & otherwise. \end{cases}$$

Note that the MAC graph is undirected, and, therefore, the simple path between two nodes *n* and *m* is counted twice, one starting from node *n* and ending at node *m* and vice versa. The impact of such duplication is eliminated in the normalized measure because the simple paths are also counted twice when calculating *NSP*(*FG*).

Example 2.24

The Java code given in Figure 2.13 shows an example class that has two methods and three attributes. The MAC graph for this class is shown in Figure 2.14. The graph has three nodes representing attributes, two nodes representing methods, and five edges representing the reference of the attributes by the methods. Figure 2.15 depicts the five all-simple-paths trees that correspond to the five nodes that are included in the MAC graph. For example, in the construction process of an all-simple-paths tree for node m_2 [Figure 2.15(e)], a corresponding node is added as a root and is marked *not final*. The three edges that are connected to node m_2 in the graph are traversed. They all lead to nodes that are not yet represented in the tree and, therefore, corresponding nodes are added as children to the tree root node; the added nodes are marked *not final*, and the root node is marked *final*. After that, each of the graph nodes that correspond to the added nodes is examined. First, graph node a_1 is examined, wherein it is found that it is connected to two nodes, m_1 and m_2. However, a node that corresponds to m_2 is already encountered in the tree path from m_2 to a_1; therefore, the node is ignored. Conversely, a node that corresponds to m_1 is not encountered in the path from m_2 to a_1; therefore, a corresponding node is added as a child for the tree node that corresponds to a_1, and the added node is marked *not final*. Now, all graph edges that are connected to node a_1 are traversed, and, therefore, the corresponding tree node is marked *final*. The process similarly continues to construct the tree.

There are eight nodes in the tree shown in Figure 2.15(a), excluding the root, which means that there are exactly eight possible simple paths that start at node a_1. Similarly, there are eight, seven, eight, and seven simple paths that start from nodes *a2*, *a3*, *m1*, and *m2*, respectively. As a result, the total number of simple paths in the MAC graph depicted in Figure 2.14 is 38. S_a and S_m for an *FG* that corresponds to the MAC graph are 14 and 12, respectively. In this case, The *NSP* for *FG* is calculated as follows.

$$NSP\left(FG_{c,\{a1,a2,a3\},\{m1,m2\}}\right) = 3 \times 14 + 2 \times 12 = 66$$

The PCCC for the class is then calculated as follows.

$$PCCC(Example_6, \{a1, a2, a3\}, \{m1, m2\}) = \frac{38}{66} = 0.576$$

```
class Example_6 {
        int a1;
        int a2;
        int a3;
        void m1(){
                a1=a2;
        }
        void m2(){
                a1=1;
                a2=a3;
        }
}
```

Figure 2.13. Java class *Example_6*

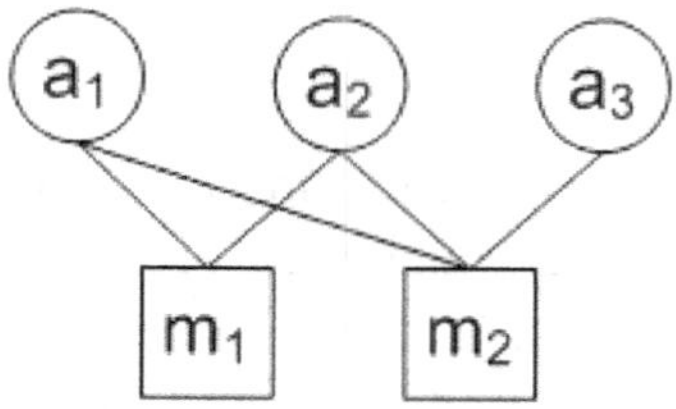

Figure 2.14. The MAC graph for class *Example_5* given in Figure 2.13.

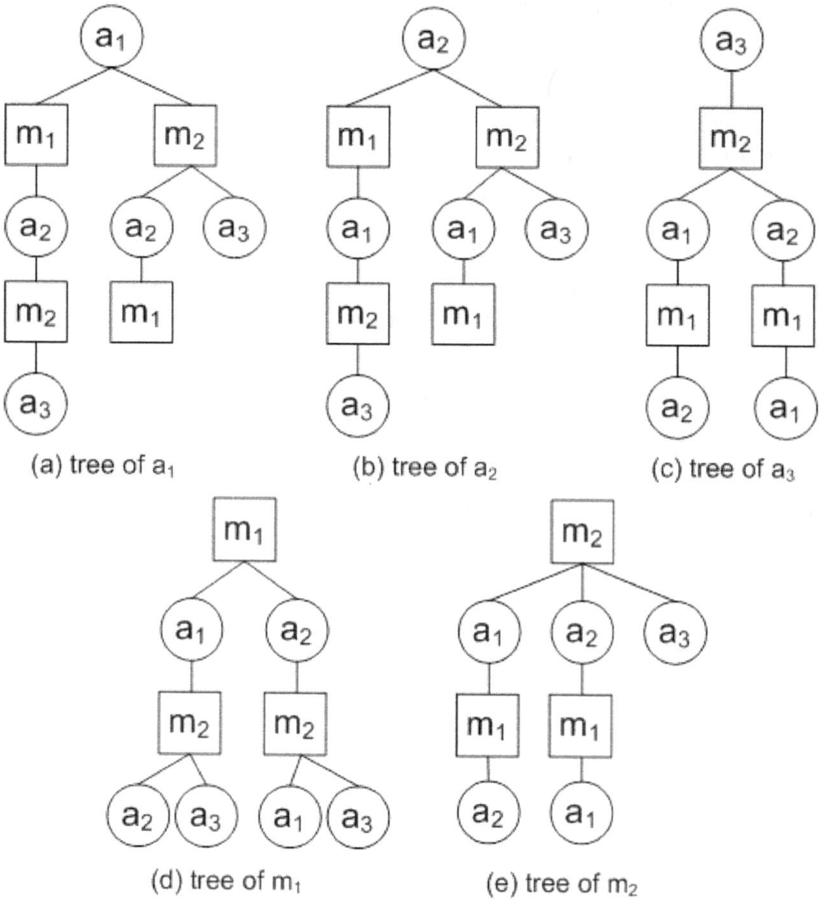

Figure 2.15. All-simple-paths trees that correspond to the nodes included in Figure 2.14.

Summary

This chapter presented definitions and descriptions of twenty class cohesion measures. Each measure is grounded in one of the models introduced in Chapter 1. Based on their underlying measurement approaches, the measures are classified into three categories: (1) those that account for the use of attributes or types, (2) those that consider the sharing of attributes or types, and (3) those that rely on graph connectivity concepts. Examples are provided to illustrate the application of each measure.

Portions of this chapter are adapted from the following papers *(reproduced with permission from the publishers)*:

- J. Al Dallal, Fault prediction and the discriminative powers of connectivity-based object-oriented class cohesion metrics, Information and Software Technology, 2012, Vol. 54, No. 4, pp. 396-416.
- J. Al Dallal and L. Briand, An object-oriented high-level design-based class cohesion metric, Information and Software Technology, 2010, Vol. 52, No. 12, pp. 1346-1361.

CHAPTER 3 COHESION MEASURE PROPERTIES

In order to increase the likelihood that a cohesion measure is well defined and serves as a good indicator for the relatedness of class members, researchers must validate the measure, both theoretically and empirically. Briand et al. (1998) propose four properties that must be satisfied by all class cohesion measures. If a measure does not satisfy any of these properties, the measure is ill defined, and its usefulness as a cohesion indicator is questionable. These properties provide a supportive underlying theory for measures. Empirical validation is necessary to show the usefulness of measures. Despite its importance, few researchers focus on the theoretical validation of measures. In this chapter, we study the validity of twenty class cohesion measures, using the properties introduced by Briand et al. (1998). We provide mathematical proofs for the measures that satisfy the cohesion properties and provide counter examples otherwise. The results show that most of the measures satisfy all or most of the properties.

3.1. Class Cohesion Measure Properties

Briand et al. (1998) define four properties for cohesion measures as follows.

Property 1: Non-negativity and normalization
The cohesion measure must belong to a specific interval [0, Max]. Normalization allows for easy comparison between the cohesion of different classes.

Property 2: Null value and maximum value
The cohesion of a class equals 0 if the class has no cohesive interactions; the cohesion is equal to Max if all possible interactions within the class are present.

Property 3: Monotonicity
Adding cohesive interactions to the module cannot decrease its cohesion.

Property 4: Cohesive modules
Merging two unrelated modules into one module does not increase the modules' cohesion. Therefore, given two classes, c_1 and c_2, the cohesion of the merged class c' must satisfy the following condition: cohesion(c') $\leq$ max {cohesion(c_1), cohesion(c_2)}. In the following discussion, the two merged classes, c_1 and c_2, are of k and m number of methods, respectively.

3.2. Satisfaction to Measure Properties

This section studies the theoretical validation of twenty class cohesion measures. The satisfaction of the four class cohesion necessary properties is proved mathematically or disproved, using a counter example.

3.2.1. Coh

Property 1 and Property 2: The minimum value for Coh is 0 when the class has no cohesive interactions. The maximum value for Coh is 1 when the class has the maximum possible number of interactions. Therefore, the measure satisfies both Property 1 and Property 2.

Property 3: Since Coh is defined as the relative number of cohesive interactions, it increases when a cohesive interaction is added to the class model. Therefore, the measure satisfies Property 3.

Property 4: To prove the Coh measure's satisfaction of Property 4, we introduce the following *numerator-denominator cohesion proving* model:

$$\frac{N(A)}{D(A)} \geq \frac{N(B)}{D(B)}$$
$$\Rightarrow D(B)N(A) \geq D(A)N(B)$$
$$\Rightarrow [D(B)+D(A)]N(A) \geq D(A)[N(A)+N(B)]$$
$$\Rightarrow \frac{N(A)}{D(A)} \geq \frac{N(A)+N(B)}{D(A)+D(B)}$$

Given the following conditions:

Condition 1: $\mathrm{N(M)} \leq \mathrm{N(A)} + \mathrm{N(B)}$
Condition 2: $\mathrm{D(M)} \geq \mathrm{D(A)} + \mathrm{D(B)}$

$$\frac{N(A)}{D(A)} \geq \frac{N(A)+N(B)}{D(A)+D(B)} \geq \frac{N(M)}{D(M)}$$

This means that max{cohesion(A), cohesion(B)} ≥ cohesion(M). Therefore, if a cohesion measure satisfies *Conditions 1* and *2*, it satisfies Property 4.

Coh is a relative measure, and, therefore, to prove its satisfaction of Property 4, we prove its satisfaction of Conditions 1 and 2 of the *numerator-denominator cohesion proving* model as follows:

When unrelated classes A and B are merged into class M, the number of interactions in M is equal to the summation of the number of interactions in classes A and B. Thus, N(M)=N(A)+N(B), which satisfies Condition 1. In addition,

$$D(M) = \frac{(k+m)(k+m-1)}{2} = \frac{k(k-1)}{2} + \frac{m(m-1)}{2} + km$$
$$= D(A) + D(B) + km \Rightarrow D(M) > D(A) + D(B)$$

This means that Coh also satisfies Condition 2, and, therefore, the measure satisfies Property 4.

3.2.2. $LCOM_H$

Property 1 and Property 2: The minimum value for $LCOM_H$ is equal to 0 when each pair of methods shares at least one common attribute (i.e., the model has the maximum number of cohesion interactions). The maximum value for $LCOM_H$ depends on the number of methods in a class. This value is defined as $k/(k-1)$, where k is the number of methods, when none of the methods share common attributes (i.e., the model does not have cohesion interactions). Therefore, $LCOM_H$ satisfies Property 2, but does not satisfy Property 1.

Property 3: The following proof shows that $LCOM_H$ satisfies Property 3.

$$LCOM_H(c') = \frac{k - \frac{1}{l}\left(1 + \sum_{i=1}^{l}\sum_{j=1}^{k} m_{ji}\right)}{k-1}$$

$$= \frac{k - \frac{1}{l}\sum_{i=1}^{l}\sum_{j=1}^{k} m_{ji}}{k-1} - \frac{1}{l(k-1)} < LCOM_H(c)$$

Property 4: In some cases, $LCOM_H$ does not satisfy Property 4. For example, given two classes A and B such that each class has two methods and two attributes, and none of the methods use any attribute, $LCOM_H(A) = LCOM_H(B) = 2$. When both classes are merged into class M, $LCOM_H(M) = (4 - 0) / (4 - 1) = 1.33$. Therefore, in this case, $LCOM_H(M) < \min\{LCOM_H(A), LCOM_H(B)\}$, which violates Property 4.

3.2.3. CAMC

Property 1 and Property 2: The minimum value for CAMC is $CAMC_{min} = (k+l-1)/kl$ when each parameter type is used by only one method, and the class type is used by all methods. The maximum value for CAMC is 1 when all methods have the same parameter types. Since the minimum value for CAMC is greater than 0, the measure does not satisfy Property 1. Since the model of the class used by CAMC cannot be free of cohesive interactions, the null and maximum value property is not applicable.

Property 3 and Property 4: CAMC is defined as the relative number of cohesive interactions in the model representing the class. Therefore, similar to Coh, CAMC satisfies the monotonicity and cohesive modules properties.

3.2.4. $LCOM_{CK1}$

Property 1 and Property 2: The minimum value for $LCOM_{CK1}$ is 0 when each pair of methods shares at least one common attribute (i.e., the model has the maximal number of cohesion interactions). The maximum value for $LCOM_{CK1}$ depends on the number of methods in a class. That is, $k(k\text{-}1)/2$, where k is the number of methods, when none of the methods share common attributes (i.e., the model does not have cohesion interactions). Therefore, $LCOM_{CK1}$ satisfies Property 2, but it does not satisfy Property 1.

Property 3: Adding a cohesive interaction to the model implies decreasing the number of unrelated pairs of methods, hence decreasing $LCOM_{CK1}$ and increasing the cohesion. Therefore, $LCOM_{CK1}$ satisfies Property 3.

Property 4: Unrelated classes are classes that have no common attributes and methods. Given that P_C and Q_C are the number of pairs of methods with and without shared attributes in a class C, for classes A, B, and M, where A and B are unrelated classes, and M is their merged class version, $Q_M = Q_A + Q_B$. The $LCOM_{CK1}$ of the merged class is calculated as follows:

$$LCOM_{CK1}(M) = P_M = \frac{(k+m)(k+m-1)}{2} - Q_M$$
$$= \frac{(k+m)(k+m-1)}{2} - [Q_A + Q_B]$$
$$= \frac{(k+m)(k+m-1)}{2} - [(P_A - \frac{k(k-1)}{2}) + (P_B - \frac{m(m-1)}{2})]$$
$$= km + P_A + P_B = km + LCOM_{CK1}(A) + LCOM_{CK1}(B)$$

The cohesion of the merged class is less than the cohesion of each of the split classes; therefore, the $LCOM_{CK1}$ measure satisfies Property 4.

3.2.5. $LCOM_{CK2}$

Property 1 and Property 2: The minimum value for $LCOM_{CK2}$ is 0 when $P_c \leq Q_c$. Therefore, when the model has the maximum number of interactions, $LCOM_{CK2}$ becomes 0 because, in this case, the number of pairs that do not share common attributes is less than those that share common attributes (i.e., $0 < k \times (k - 1) / 2$). However, the maximum value for $LCOM_{CK2}$ depends on the number of methods in a class. That is, $k \times (k-1)/2$, where k is the number of methods, when none of the methods share common attributes (i.e., the model does not have cohesion interactions). Therefore, $LCOM_{CK2}$ satisfies Property 2, but does not satisfy Property 1.

Property 3: Adding a cohesive interaction to the model implies increasing Q and decreasing P. If, in the original model, $P_c \leq Q_c$, the cohesion of the original and the modified models equal 0. Otherwise, $LCOM_{CK2}$ of the model decreases. Therefore, $LCOM_{CK2}$ satisfies Property 3.

Property 4: When two unrelated classes are merged,

$$LCOM_{CK2}(M) = P_M - Q_M = (km + P_A + P_B) - (Q_A + Q_B)$$
$$= km + (P_A - Q_A) + (P_B - Q_B)$$
$$= km + LCOM_{CK2}(A) + LCOM_{CK2}(B)$$

The cohesion of the merged class is less than the cohesion of each of the split classes; therefore, the $LCOM_{CK2}$ measure satisfies Property 4.

3.2.6. TCC

Property 1 and Property 2: The minimum value for TCC is 0 when the class has no cohesive interactions. The maximum value for TCC is 1 when the class has the maximum possible number of interactions. Therefore, the measure satisfies both Property 1 and Property 2.

Property 3: Since TCC is defined as the relative number of cohesive interactions, it increases when a cohesive interaction is added to the class model. Therefore, the measure satisfies Property 3.

Property 4: TCC is a relative measure, and, therefore, to prove its satisfaction of Property 4, we prove its satisfaction of Conditions 1 and 2 of the *numerator-denominator cohesion proving* model as follows:

When unrelated classes A and B are merged into class M, the number of interactions in M is equal to the summation of the number of interactions in classes A and B. Thus, N(M) = N(A) + N(B), which satisfies Condition 1. In addition,

$$D(M) = \frac{(k+m)(k+m-1)}{2} = \frac{k(k-1)}{2} + \frac{m(m-1)}{2} + km$$
$$= D(A) + D(B) + km \Rightarrow D(M) > D(A) + D(B)$$

Therefore, TCC satisfies Condition 2. As a result, TCC satisfies Property 4.

3.2.7. LCC

Property 1 and Property 2: The minimum value for LCC is 0 when the class has no cohesive interactions. The maximum value for LCC is 1 when the class has the maximum possible number of interactions. Therefore, the measure satisfies both Property 1 and Property 2.

Property 3: Since LCC is defined as the relative number of cohesive interactions, it increases when a cohesive interaction is added to the class model. Therefore, the measure satisfies Property 3.

Property 4: LCC is a relative measure, and, therefore, to prove its satisfaction of Property 4, we prove its satisfaction of Conditions 1 and 2 of the *numerator-denominator cohesion proving* model as follows:

When unrelated classes A and B are merged into class M, the number of interactions in M is equal to the summation of the number of interactions in classes A and B. Thus, N(M) = N(A) + N(B), which satisfies Condition 1. In addition,

$$D(M) = \frac{(k+m)(k+m-1)}{2} = \frac{k(k-1)}{2} + \frac{m(m-1)}{2} + km$$

$$= D(A) + D(B) + km \Rightarrow D(M) > D(A) + D(B)$$

Therefore, LCC satisfies Condition 2. As a result, LCC satisfies Property 4.

3.2.8. DC_D

Property 1 and Property 2: The minimum value for DC_D is 0 when the class has no cohesive interactions. The maximum value for DC_D is 1 when the class has the maximum possible number of interactions. Therefore, the measure satisfies both Property 1 and Property 2.

Property 3: Since DC_D is defined as the relative number of cohesive interactions, it increases when a cohesive interaction is added to the class model. Therefore, the measure satisfies Property 3.

Property 4: DC_D is a relative measure, and, therefore, to prove its satisfaction of Property 4, we prove its satisfaction of Conditions 1 and 2 of the *numerator-denominator cohesion proving* model as follows:

When unrelated classes A and B are merged into class M, the number of interactions in M is equal to the summation of the number of interactions in classes A and B. Thus, N(M) = N(A) + N(B), which satisfies Condition 1. In addition,

$$D(M) = \frac{(k+m)(k+m-1)}{2} = \frac{k(k-1)}{2} + \frac{m(m-1)}{2} + km$$
$$= D(A) + D(B) + km \Rightarrow D(M) > D(A) + D(B)$$

Therefore, DC_D satisfies Condition 2. As a result, DC_D satisfies Property 4.

3.2.9. DC_I

Property 1 and Property 2: The minimum value for DC_I is 0 when the class has no cohesive interactions. The maximum value for DC_I is 1 when the class has the maximum possible number of interactions. Therefore, the measure satisfies both Property 1 and Property 2.

Property 3: Since DC_I is defined as the relative number of cohesive interactions, it increases when a cohesive interaction is added to the class model. Therefore, the measure satisfies Property 3.

Property 4: DC_I is a relative measure, and, therefore, to prove its satisfaction of Property 4, we prove its satisfaction of Conditions 1 and 2 of the *numerator-denominator cohesion proving* model as follows:

When unrelated classes A and B are merged into class M, the number of interactions in M is equal to the summation of the number of interactions in classes A and B. Thus, N(M) = N(A) + N(B), which satisfies Condition 1. In addition,

$$D(M) = \frac{(k+m)(k+m-1)}{2} = \frac{k(k-1)}{2} + \frac{m(m-1)}{2} + km$$
$$= D(A) + D(B) + km \Rightarrow D(M) > D(A) + D(B)$$

Therefore, DC_I satisfies Condition 2. As a result, DC_I satisfies Property 4.

3.2.10. CC

Property 1 and Property 2: The minimum value for CC equals 0 when none of the methods share common attributes, which includes the case in which none of the methods use any attribute (i.e., the model does not have any cohesive interaction). The maximum value for CC is 1 when all methods share the same set of attributes, which includes the case in which all methods share all attributes (i.e., the model has all possible cohesive interactions). Therefore, the CC measure satisfies both non-negativity and normalization, as well as null and maximum value cohesion properties.

Property 3: CC does not satisfy Property 3 in some cases. That is, when a cohesive interaction is added to a class, the counterintuitive result may be a class with a lower CC value, as depicted in classes C and D, shown in Figure 3.1. This occurs because the addition of a cohesive interaction may increase the similarities between pairs of methods and decrease the similarities between other pairs of methods. In this case, the cohesion increases if the summation of the similarities between pairs of methods increases, and vice versa.

Property 4: When two unrelated classes A and B are merged into class M, the similarity between each pair of methods in class A and class B does not change. This is because the similarity of a pair of methods is defined as the ratio of the number of shared attributes between both methods to the number of attributes used by both methods. These two numbers remain the same in class M. Since classes A and B are unrelated, no similarities exist between methods in class A and methods in class B. Therefore, N(M) = N(A) + N(B) (i.e., CC satisfies Condition 1). CC also satisfies Condition 2 (the proof is identical to the corresponding one given for the Coh measure). As a result, CC satisfies the cohesive modules property.

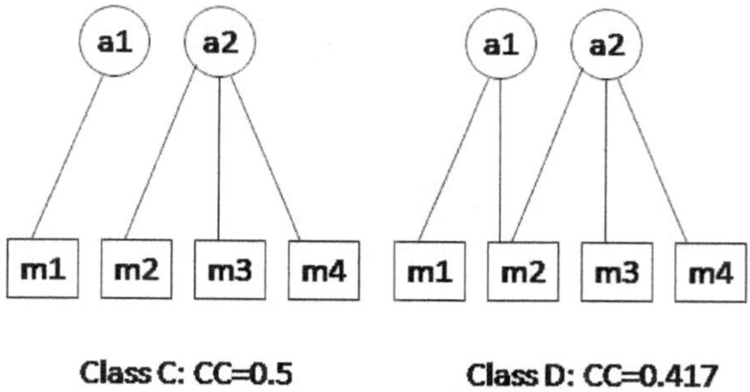

Figure 3.1. Violation of CC in terms of monotonicity

3.2.11. SCOM

Property 1 and Property 2: The minimum value for SCOM is equal to 0 when none of the methods share common attributes, which includes the case in which none of the methods use any attribute (i.e., the model does not have any cohesive interaction). The maximum value for SCOM is 1 when all methods share all attributes (i.e., the model has all possible cohesive interactions). Therefore, the SCOM measure satisfies both non-negativity and normalization, as well as null and maximum value cohesion properties.

Property 3: In some cases, when a cohesive interaction is added to the model, the SCOM value of the class decreases to some extent. Figure 3.2 shows an example (classes A and B) for which the measure violates Property 3. This decrease is due to the fact that, in SCOM, the similarity is inversely proportional to the minimum number of attributes used in both methods. In some cases, adding a cohesive interaction increases this number and, consequently, decreases the similarity between some pairs of methods. When this decrease is greater than the increase of the similarity between some other pairs of methods in the class, the SCOM value decreases.

Property 4: To use our *numerator-denominator cohesion proving* model, we adjust the definition of similarity as follows:

$$SS(i,j)=\frac{|I_i \cap I_j|}{\min(|I_i|,|I_j|)}\cdot\frac{|I_i \cup I_j|}{l}=\frac{s_{ij}}{l}$$

Therefore, $SCOM(C)=\dfrac{\sum_{i=1}^{k-1}\sum_{j=i+1}^{k}SS(i,j)}{\frac{k(k-1)}{2}}=\dfrac{\sum_{i=1}^{k-1}\sum_{j=i+1}^{k}s_{ij}}{\frac{lk(k-1)}{2}}=\dfrac{N(C)}{D(C)}$

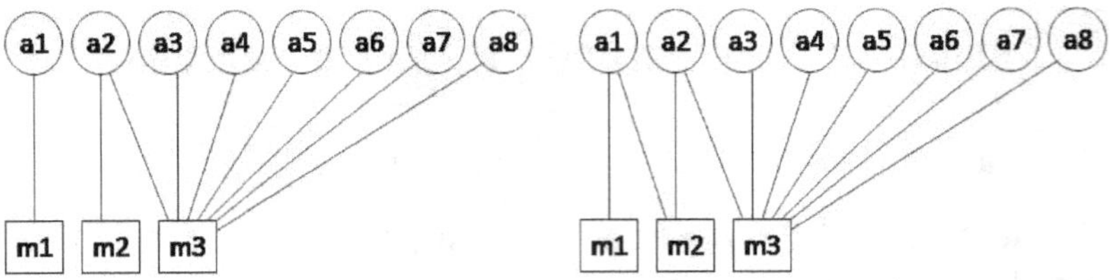

Class A: SCOM=0.292 Class B: SCOM=0.25

Figure 3.2. Violation of SCOM in terms of monotonicity

When two unrelated classes A and B are merged into class M, s_{ij} between each pair of methods in class A and class B, does not change, because none of the parameters on which the s_{ij} value depends change. Since classes A and B are unrelated, s_{ij} between any method in class A and any method in class B equals 0 because none of the attributes are shared between the methods. Therefore, N(M) = N(A) + N(B) (i.e., satisfies Condition 1). The following proof shows that SCOM satisfies Condition 2.

$$D(M)=0.5[(l+n)(k+m)(k+m-1)]=0.5lk(k-1)$$
$$+0.5nm(m-1)+0.5[(lm+nk)(k+m-1)+m(lk+nk)]$$
$$=D(A)+D(B)+0.5[(lm+nk)(k+m-1)+m(lk+nk)]$$
$$>D(A)+D(B)$$

As a result, SCOM satisfies the cohesive modules property.

3.2.12. LSCC

Property 1: The minimum value for the LSCC measure for a class is 0 when the class has either (1) several methods and no attributes or (2) several methods such that none of their pairs share a common attribute. The maximum value for the LSCC measure for a class is 1 when the class has (1) one or more attributes and no methods, (2) one method, or (3) several methods and one or more attributes with each pair of methods sharing all attributes in the class (i.e., each method references all attributes in the class). As a result, the LSCC measure ranges over the interval [0, 1], and it therefore complies with the non-negativity and normalization property.

Property 2: Given a class with a set of methods and attributes, if none of the pairs of methods share a common attribute (that is, the class has no method-method interactions), the value of the LSCC measure will be 0. Alternatively, if each attribute is shared between each pair of methods (that is, the class features all possible method-method interactions), the value of the LSCC measure will be 1 (that is, the maximum possible value). Hence, the LSCC measure complies with the null and maximum values property.

Property 3: The addition of a method-method interaction to the IMA matrix is represented by changing an entry value from 0 to 1 in a column that has at least one entry value of 1. Changing such an entry value from 0 to 1 increases the number of 1s in the column, which increases the numerator value in the alternative LSCC formula given in Section 2.2.9. An increase in the numerator in this formula increases the value of the LSCC measure, because the denominator does not change unless the size of the matrix changes. As a result, the addition of a cohesive interaction represented in the IMA matrix always increases the LSCC value, which means that the LSCC measure complies with the monotonicity property.

Property 4: The merging of two unrelated classes *c1* and *c2* implies that none of the methods in each of the two classes are shared and that none of them share common attributes. Therefore, the number of rows and columns in the IMA matrix of the merged class equals the sum of the number of rows and columns in the IMA matrices of the unrelated classes. The number of 1s in each column in the IMA matrix of the merged class equals the number of 1s in the corresponding column in the IMA matrices of the unrelated classes. Therefore, for the IMA $k \times l$ matrix representing class *c1*, the IMA $m \times n$ matrix representing class *c2*, and the IMA $(k+m) \times (l+n)$ matrix representing the merged class *c3*:

$$\sum_{i=1}^{l} x_i(x_i-1) + \sum_{i=1}^{n} x_i(x_i-1) = \sum_{i=1}^{l+n} x_i(x_i-1)$$

Suppose that LSCC(*c1*)≥LSCC(*c2*), then:

$$\frac{\sum_{i=1}^{l} x_i(x_i-1)}{lk(k-1)} \geq \frac{\sum_{i=1}^{n} x_i(x_i-1)}{mn(m-1)} \Rightarrow mn(m-1)\sum_{i=1}^{l} x_i(x_i-1) \geq lk(k-1)\sum_{i=1}^{n} x_i(x_i-1)$$

$$\Rightarrow [mn(m-1)+lk(k-1)]\sum_{i=1}^{l} x_i(x_i-1) \geq lk(k-1)[\sum_{i=1}^{n} x_i(x_i-1) + \sum_{i=1}^{l} x_i(x_i-1)]$$

$$\Rightarrow \frac{\sum_{i=1}^{l} x_i(x_i-1)}{lk(k-1)} \geq \frac{\sum_{i=1}^{n} x_i(x_i-1) + \sum_{i=1}^{l} x_i(x_i-1)}{mn(m-1)+lk(k-1)} >$$

$$\frac{\sum_{i=1}^{n} x_i(x_i-1) + \sum_{i=1}^{l} x_i(x_i-1)}{mn(m-1)+lk(k-1)+(l+n)km+(lm+nk)(k+m-1)}$$

$$\Rightarrow \frac{\sum_{i=1}^{l} x_i(x_i-1)}{lk(k-1)} > \frac{\sum_{i=1}^{l+n} x_i(x_i-1)}{(l+n)(m+k)(k+m-1)} \Rightarrow LSCC(c1) > LSCC(c3)$$

So, *Max*{LSCC(*c1*),LSCC(*c2*)} > LSCC(*c3*). This means that the LSCC measure complies with the cohesive module property.

3.2.13. NHD

Property 1 and Property 2: The NHD measure has the minimum value when each column in the matrix that models the class has the maximum possible disagreements, by setting $x_i = \frac{k}{2}$ in the alternative NHD formula given in Section 2.2.10. In this case, $NHD_{min} = \frac{k-2}{2\times(k-1)}$. The maximum value for NHD is equal to 1 when the matrix contains only 1s (i.e., the class has all possible interactions). Since the minimum value for NHD is greater than 0, the measure does not satisfy Property 1. Since the model of the class used by NHD cannot be free of cohesive interactions, the *null and maximum value* property is not applicable.

Property 3: Adding a cohesive interaction to the class is represented in the matrix by changing two entries in a column in the matrix from 0 to 1 if neither method used the parameter type, or changing one entry from 0 to 1 if one of the methods was using the parameter type. If a column n in the matrix has $x_n > \frac{k}{2}$, where x_n is the number of 1s in the column, according to the NHD formula, the value of NHD after adding the cohesive interaction is less than it was before adding the cohesive interaction, which violates Property 3.

Property 4: In some cases, NHD violates the cohesive modules property. For example, consider two classes, A and B, where each has two methods: one of the methods has two parameter types, and the other method does not have any parameter types. In this case, the cohesion of each class is equal to 0. When the two classes are merged, the new matrix is 4×4, and the NHD value of the merged class is 0.5, which is greater than the NHD value of each of classes A and B.

3.2.14. MMAC

Property 1: The minimum value for the MMAC measure for a class is 0 when the class has either (1) no methods, (2) no attributes, or (3) several methods such that none of their pairs share a common attribute type. The maximum value for the MMAC measure for a class is 1 when the class has (1) one method or (2) several methods and one or more attributes with each pair of methods sharing all attribute types in the class (i.e., each method has all distinct attribute types as types for its parameters). As a result, the MMAC measure ranges over the interval [0, 1], and it therefore complies with the non-negativity and normalization property.

Property 2: Given a class with a set of methods and attributes, if none of the pairs of methods share a common attribute type, the value of the MMAC measure will be 0. Alternatively, if each attribute type is shared between each pair of methods (that is, the class features all possible method-method interactions), the value of the MMAC measure will be 1 (that is, the maximum possible value). Hence, the MMAC measure complies with the null and maximum values property.

Property 3: The addition of a method-method interaction to the IAT matrix is represented by changing an entry value from 0 to 1 in a column that has at least one entry value of 1. Changing such an entry value from 0 to 1 increases the number of 1s in the column, which increases the numerator value in the alternative MMAC formula given in Section 2.2.11. An increase in the numerator in this formula increases the value of the MMAC measure, because the denominator does not change unless the size of the matrix changes. As a result, the addition of a cohesive interaction represented in the IAT matrix always increases the MMAC value, which means that the MMAC measure complies with the monotonicity property.

Property 4: The merging of two unrelated classes *c1* and *c2* implies that none of the methods in each of the two classes are shared and that none of them share common attribute types. Therefore, the number of rows and columns in the IAT matrix of the merged class equals the sum of the number of rows and columns in the IAT matrices of the unrelated classes. The number of 1s in each column in the IAT matrix of the merged class equals the number of 1s in the corresponding column in the IAT matrices of the unrelated classes. Therefore, for the IAT $k \times l$ matrix representing class *c1*, the IAT $m \times n$ matrix representing class *c2*, and the IAT $(k + m) \times (l + n)$ matrix representing the merged class *c3*:

$$\sum_{i=1}^{l} x_i(x_i - 1) + \sum_{i=1}^{n} x_i(x_i - 1) = \sum_{i=1}^{l+n} x_i(x_i - 1)$$

Suppose that MMAC(*c1*) ≥ MMAC(*c2*), then:

$$\frac{\sum_{i=1}^{l} x_i(x_i-1)}{lk(k-1)} \geq \frac{\sum_{i=1}^{n} x_i(x_i-1)}{mn(m-1)} \Rightarrow mn(m-1)\sum_{i=1}^{l} x_i(x_i-1) \geq lk(k-1)\sum_{i=1}^{n} x_i(x_i-1)$$

$$\Rightarrow [mn(m-1)+lk(k-1)]\sum_{i=1}^{l} x_i(x_i-1) \geq lk(k-1)[\sum_{i=1}^{n} x_i(x_i-1)+\sum_{i=1}^{l} x_i(x_i-1)]$$

$$\Rightarrow \frac{\sum_{i=1}^{l} x_i(x_i-1)}{lk(k-1)} \geq \frac{\sum_{i=1}^{n} x_i(x_i-1)+\sum_{i=1}^{l} x_i(x_i-1)}{mn(m-1)+lk(k-1)} >$$

$$\frac{\sum_{i=1}^{n} x_i(x_i-1)+\sum_{i=1}^{l} x_i(x_i-1)}{mn(m-1)+lk(k-1)+(l+n)km+(lm+nk)(k+m-1)}$$

$$\Rightarrow \frac{\sum_{i=1}^{l} x_i(x_i-1)}{lk(k-1)} > \frac{\sum_{i=1}^{l+n} x_i(x_i-1)}{(l+n)(m+k)(k+m-1)} \Rightarrow MMAC(c1) > MMAC(c3)$$

So, Max\{MMAC(*c1*),MMAC(*c2*)\} > MMAC(*c3*). This means that the MMAC measure complies with the cohesive module property.

3.2.15. LCOM$_L$

Property 1 and Property 2: The minimum value for LCOM$_L$ is 1 when there is a direct or indirect cohesive interaction between each method and another. The maximum value for LCOM$_L$ depends on the number of methods in a class (i.e., k, where k is the number of methods, when the model has no interactions). The value of LCOM$_L$ ranges in the interval [1, k], and, therefore, the measure does not satisfy Property 1. In addition, the measure does not satisfy Property 2 because the value of LCOM$_L$ is not equal to 0 when the model has the maximum possible interactions.

Property 3: When adding a cohesive interaction to the model, the number of connected components either decreases by 1, when the interaction connects two disjoint components, or remains the same, when the interaction does not connect two disjoint components. Therefore, LCOM$_L$ satisfies Property 3.

Property 4: Two unrelated classes are graphically represented by two disjoint graphs. Therefore, when two unrelated classes A and B are merged into class M, the total number of disjoint components increases by 1 (i.e., $LCOM_L(M) = LCOM_L(A) + LCOM_L(B) + 1$). Hence, the $LCOM_L$ measure satisfies Property 4.

3.2.16. $LCOM_{HM}$

The only difference between $LCOM_{HM}$ and $LCOM_L$ is in the definition of the cohesive interactions. The discussion about the validity of $LCOM_L$, given in Section 3.2.14, is independent from the definition of the cohesive interactions, and, therefore, both measures have the same properties. However, when the graph is connected (i.e., $LCOM_{HM} = 1$), the connectivity measure is used. The satisfaction of the connectivity measure to the properties is discussed as follows.

Property 1 and Property 2: The connectivity measure is defined only for the cases where $LCOM_{HM}$ is equal to 1. When $LCOM_{HM}$ equals 1, the graph that represents the class is connected, and the number of edges in the graph is not less than k-1. The minimum value for the connectivity measure is equal to 0 when the model to which the measure can be applied has the minimum possible number of interactions. The maximum value for connectivity is equal to 1 when the model has the maximum possible number of interactions (i.e., $e = k\times(k-1)/2$). Therefore, the connectivity measure satisfies Property 1 when it is applied to the models for which it is defined. However, a combination of $LCOM_{HM}$ and connectivity does not satisfy Property 1. Property 2 is not applicable for the connectivity measure because the measure is undefined when the model of the class has no interactions. The combination of $LCOM_{HM}$ and connectivity satisfies Property 2 because connectivity solves the problem of the maximum value.

Property 3: Adding a cohesive interaction to the class implies adding an edge to the models that represent the class. The connectivity value increases, and, therefore, the measure satisfies Property 3. Hence, the combination of $LCOM_{HM}$ and connectivity satisfies Property 3.

Property 4: When two unrelated classes are merged, the model of the resulting class will have the number of edges equal to the summation of the number of edges in the models of both classes (i.e., $e_M = e_A + e_B$). The connectivity measure is proved to satisfy the cohesive modules property as follows.

$$N(M) = 2(e_M - (k+m-1)) = 2e_M - 2(k+m-1)$$
$$= 2(e_A + e_B) - 2(k+m-1)$$
$$= 2(e_A - (k-1)) + 2(e_B - (m-1)) - 2$$
$$= N(A) + N(B) - 2 < N(A) + N(B)$$
$$D(M) = (k+m-1)(k+m-2)$$
$$= (k-1)(k-2) + (m-1)(m-2) + m(k-1) +$$
$$k(m-1) + (k+m-2)$$
$$> (k-1)(k-2) + (m-1)(m-2) = D(A) + D(B)$$

The measure satisfies Conditions 1 and 2 of the *numerator-denominator cohesion proving* model given in Section 3.2.1, and, therefore, it satisfies Property 4. Hence, the combination of $LCOM_{HM}$ and connectivity satisfies Property 4.

3.2.17. CBMC

Property 1: The minimum value for the CBMC measure for a class is 0 when the MAC graph that represents the class is disjoint. The maximum value for the CBMC measure for a class is 1 when each of the methods in the class of interest references each attribute. As a result, the CBMC measure ranges over the interval [0, 1], and it therefore complies with the non-negativity and normalization property.

Property 2: Given a class with a set of methods and attributes, if none of the methods references an attribute, the value of the CBMC measure will be 0. Alternatively, if each attribute is referenced by each method (that is, the class features all possible method-attribute interactions), the value of the CBMC measure will be 1 (that is, the maximum possible value). Hence, the CBMC measure complies with the null and maximum values property.

Property 3: CBMC does not satisfy Property 3 in some cases. That is, when a cohesive interaction is added to a class, the counterintuitive result may be a class with a lower CBMC value, as depicted in classes C and D, shown in Figure 3.3. In this example, the value of CBMC for class C equals $\frac{2}{4} \times \frac{1+1+1}{3} = \frac{1}{2}$. When adding a cohesive interaction to class C forming class D, the value of the CBMC is decreased to $\frac{2}{4} \times \frac{1+\frac{1}{2}\times\frac{1+1}{2}}{2} = \frac{3}{8}$.

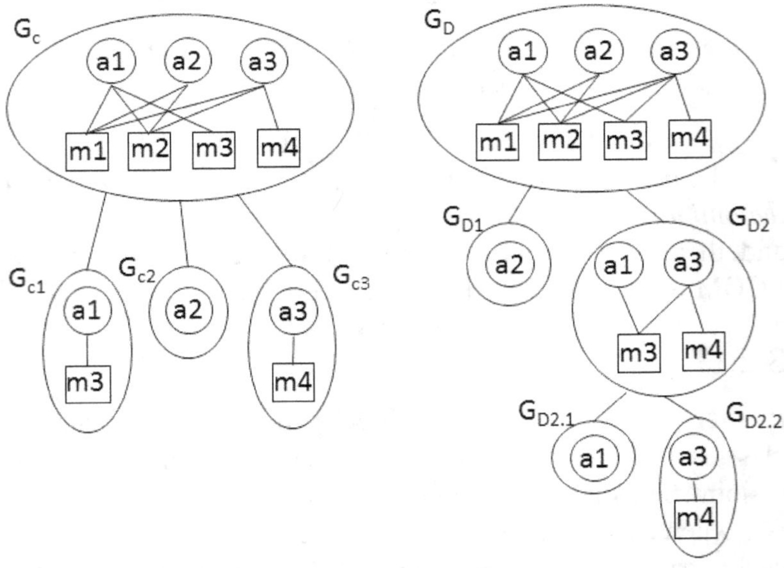

Figure 3.3. Application of CBMC to hypothetical classes

Property 4: The merging of two unrelated classes *c1* and *c2* implies forming a class that its MAC graph is disjoint. Therefore, the CBMC of the merged class equals zero. As a result, CBMC satisfies Property 4 because merging two unrelated modules into one module does not increase the modules' CBMC value.

3.2.18. ICBMC

Property 1: The minimum value for the ICBMC measure for a class is 0 when the MAC graph that represents the class is disjoint. The maximum value for the ICBMC measure for a class is 1 when each of the methods in the class of interest references each attribute. As a result, the ICBMC measure ranges over the interval [0, 1], and it therefore complies with the non-negativity and normalization property.

Property 2: Given a class with a set of methods and attributes, if none of the methods references an attribute, the value of the ICBMC measure will be 0. Alternatively, if each attribute is referenced by each method (that is, the class features all possible method-attribute interactions), the value of the ICBMC measure will be 1 (that is, the maximum possible value). Hence, the ICBMC measure complies with the null and maximum values property.

Property 3: ICBMC does not satisfy Property 3 in some cases. That is, when a cohesive interaction is added to a class, the counterintuitive result may be a class with a lower ICBMC value, as depicted in classes *c* and *d*, shown in Figure 3.4. In this example, the value of ICBMC for class *d* equals $\frac{1}{3\times3} \times \frac{1+1}{2} = \frac{1}{9} = 0.111$. When adding a cohesive interaction to class *d* forming class *c*, the value of the CBMC is decreased to 0.083 (as calculated for Example 2.22 in Section 2.3.4).

Property 4: The merging of two unrelated classes *c1* and *c2* implies forming a class that its MAC graph is disjoint. Therefore, the ICBMC of the merged class equals zero. As a result, ICBMC satisfies Property 4 because merging two unrelated modules into one module does not increase the modules' ICBMC value.

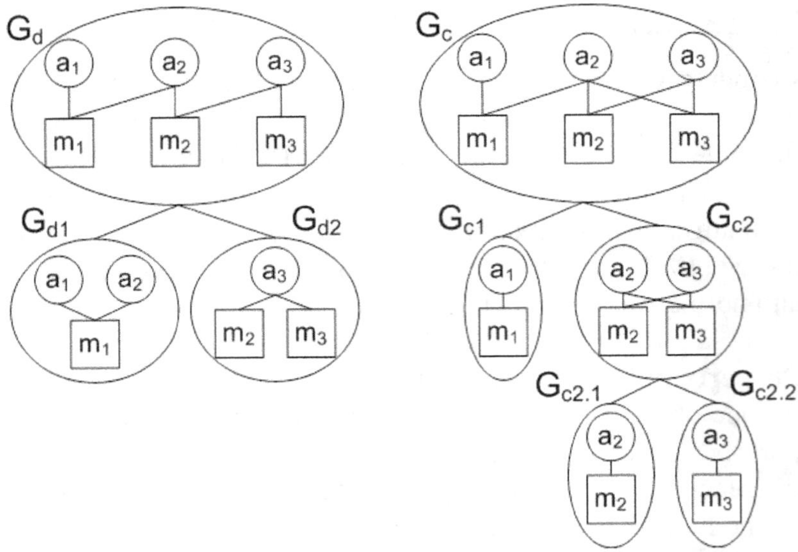

Figure 3.4. Application of ICBMC to hypothetical classes

3.2.19. OL_n

Property 1: The minimum value for the OL_n measure for a class is 0 when the MAC graph that represents the class is disjoint. The maximum value for the OL_n measure for a class is 1 when each of the methods in the class of interest references each attribute. As a result, the OL_n measure ranges over the interval [0, 1], and it therefore complies with the non-negativity and normalization property.

Property 2: Given a class with a set of methods and attributes, if none of the methods references an attribute, the value of the OL_n measure will be 0 (the MAC graph is disjoint). Alternatively, if each attribute is referenced by each method (that is, the class features all possible method-attribute interactions), the value of the OL_n measure will be 1 (that is, the maximum possible value). Hence, the OL_n measure complies with the null and maximum values property.

Property 3: Adding a cohesive interaction to the MAC graph implies increasing the S_a value for one of the attributes and does not affect the S_a value for any of the remaining attributes. Given the fact that the value of OL_n is defined as the average value of S_a for all attributes, an increase of an S_a value for one of the attributes causes the OL_n value to increase. The only exception is when the graph before and after adding the cohesive interaction is disjoint. In this case, the OL_n value remains zero. As a result, adding a cohesive interaction to the MAC graph does not cause the OL_n value to decrease, and therefore, the OL_n measure satisfies Property 3.

Property 4: The merging of two unrelated classes *c1* and *c2* implies forming a class that its MAC graph is disjoint. Therefore, the OL_n of the merged class equals zero. As a result, OL_n satisfies Property 4 because merging two unrelated modules into one module does not increase the modules' OL_n value.

3.2.20. PCCC

Property 1: The minimum value for the PCCC of a class is zero when the MAC graph of the class has no edges. In this case, none of the methods reference an attribute. The maximum value for the PCCC of a class is one when there is an edge between each node that represents an attribute and each node that represents a method in the MAC graph of the class. In this case, each method references each attribute in the class. As a result, the PCCC measure ranges over the interval [0, 1] and therefore satisfies the non-negativity and normalization property.

Property 2: Given a class with a set of methods and attributes, if none of the methods reference an attribute (that is, the class has no interactions), the PCCC value will be zero. Alternatively, if each attribute is referenced by each method (that is, the class features all possible interactions), the PCCC value will be one (that is, the maximum possible value). Hence, the PCCC measure satisfies the null-and-maximum-values property.

Property 3: The addition of an edge to the MAC graph does not break any of the simple paths, and it adds at least one more simple path of length one, which is the direct path between the two endpoint nodes of the added edge. As a result, the addition of a cohesive interaction to the class always increases the PCCC value, which means that the PCCC measure satisfies the monotonicity property.

Property 4: The merging of two unrelated classes *c1* and *c2* into class *c3* implies that none of the nodes in the MAC graph of *c1* is connected by an edge to any node in the MAC graph of *c2*. This means that $NSP(G_{c3}) = NSP(G_{c1}) + NSP(G_{c2})$. However, the fully connected graph FG_{c3} has the same set of edges in FG_{c1} and FG_{c2} in addition to the set of edges between each node in FG_{c1} and each node in FG_{c2}. This implies that $NSP(FG_{c3}) = NSP(FG_{c1}) + NSP(FG_{c2}) + f$, where f is the number of simple paths that are created by the additional edges. The value of f is zero when both classes only have attributes or methods; otherwise, the value of f is greater than zero.
Suppose that PCCC(*c1*) ≥ PCCC(*c2*); then:

$$\frac{NSP(G_{c1})}{NSP(FG_{c1})} \geq \frac{NSP(G_{c2})}{NSP(FG_{c2})} \Rightarrow NSP(G_{c1}) \times NSP(FG_{c2}) \geq$$

$$NSP(G_{c2}) \times NSP(FG_{c1})$$

$$\Rightarrow NSP(G_{c1}) \times [NSP(FG_{c1}) + NSP(FG_{c2})] \geq$$

$$[NSP(G_{c1}) + NSP(G_{c2})] \times NSP(FG_{c1})$$

$$\Rightarrow \frac{NSP(G_{c1})}{NSP(FG_{c1})} \geq \frac{NSP(G_{c1}) + NSP(G_{c2})}{NSP(FG_{c1}) + NSP(FG_{c2})} \geq$$

$$\frac{NSP(G_{c1}) + NSP(G_{c2})}{NSP(FG_{c1}) + NSP(FG_{c2}) + f}$$

$$\Rightarrow PCCC(c1) > PCCC(c3)$$

Therefore, *Max*{PCCC(*c1*),PCCC(*c2*)} > PCCC(*c3*). This means that the PCCC measure satisfies Property 4.

Summary

This chapter shows how to prove or disprove the satisfaction of class cohesion measures to the necessary properties for class cohesion. Table 3.1 summarizes the results found in this chapter.

Table 3.1. Summary of the theoretical validation results

ID	Measure	Property 1	Property 2	Property 3	Property 4
1	**Coh**	Yes	Yes	Yes	Yes
2	**$LCOM_H$**	No	Yes	Yes	No
3	**CAMC**	No	N.A.	Yes	Yes
4	**$LCOM_{CK1}$**	No	Yes	Yes	Yes
5	**$LCOM_{CK2}$**	No	Yes	Yes	Yes
6	**TCC**	Yes	Yes	Yes	Yes
7	**LCC**	Yes	Yes	Yes	Yes
8	**DC_D**	Yes	Yes	Yes	Yes
9	**DC_I**	Yes	Yes	Yes	Yes
10	**CC**	Yes	Yes	No	Yes
11	**SCOM**	Yes	Yes	No	Yes
12	**LSCC**	Yes	Yes	Yes	Yes
13	**NHD**	No	N.A.	No	No
14	**MMAC**	Yes	Yes	Yes	Yes
15	**$LCOM_L$**	No	No	Yes	Yes
16	**$LCOM_{HM}$**	No	Yes	Yes	Yes
17	**CBMC**	Yes	Yes	No	Yes
18	**ICBMC**	Yes	Yes	No	Yes
19	**OL_n**	Yes	Yes	Yes	Yes
20	**PCCC**	Yes	Yes	Yes	Yes

The results show that among the considered class cohesion measures:

- Nine (45%) measures satisfy all properties.
- Seven (35%) measures satisfy only three properties.
- Three (15%) measures satisfy only two properties.
- One (5%) measure does not satisfy any property.
- Thirteen (65%) measures satisfy Property 1.
- Seventeen (85%) measures satisfy Property 2.
- Fifteen (75%) measures satisfy Property 3.
- Eighteen (90%) measures satisfy Property 4.

In general, this means that 45% of the considered measures are valid from the theoretical perspective. All other measures must be revised to comply with the class cohesion properties. Otherwise, use of these measures as cohesion indicators is questionable.

Portions of this chapter are adapted from the following paper *(reproduced with permission from the publishers)*:

- J. Al Dallal, Mathematical validation of object-oriented class cohesion metrics, International Journal of Computers, 2010, Vol. 4, No. 2, pp. 45-52.
- J. Al Dallal, Fault prediction and the discriminative powers of connectivity-based object-oriented class cohesion metrics, Information and Software Technology, 2012, Vol. 54, No. 4, pp. 396-416.

CHAPTER 4 ADVANCED TOPICS

4.1. Accounting for Cohesion Measure Applicability

4.1.1. Motivation

Although there is no upper limit to the number of attributes and methods in a class, developers are encouraged not to develop large classes, to increase the understandability, manageability, and maintainability of their code. However, relatively large portions of object-oriented systems are composed of small classes that consist of a single attribute or a single method. Unfortunately, most class cohesion measures are undefined for one or more of these cases, i.e., cases in which a class has no attributes or parameter types, or consists of a single attribute or method, which limits the applicability and usability of these measures for a relatively large percentage of classes. For instance, $LCOM_{CK1}$, $LCOM_{CK2}$, TCC, LCC, DC_D, DC_I, CC, SCOM, $LCOM_H$, and NHD are undefined for classes consisting of fewer than two methods. In addition, $LCOM_{CK1}$, $LCOM_{CK2}$, TCC, LCC, DC_D, DC_I, CC, SCOM, $LCOM_H$, Coh, CAMC, and NHD are undefined for classes that do not contain any attributes. Finally, NHD is inapplicable for classes in which none of the methods has parameters. Limiting the applicability of these measures to certain classes may well discourage software developers from applying such measures to assess the quality of their classes. In addition, such limitation can result in unrepresentative overall quality indicator values for the system under consideration, which in turn may decrease confidence in the overall quality of the system because the developers may have no knowledge regarding the cohesion of a large portion of the system. Several empirical validation studies excluded all classes that feature cases for which the considered measures are undefined. Yet, if the measures have defined values for these classes, including them in the empirical studies could greatly alter the validation results, either positively or negatively because the percentage of classes that feature cases for which the considered measures are undefined is typically high in object-oriented systems. This limitation suggests a need to assign cohesion values to special cases in which some of the measures are undefined. These assigned values must be validated to verify that they do not cause the measures to violate key cohesion properties (e.g., the properties proposed by Briand et al. 1998).

Most of the existing cohesion measures have undefined values for classes in several special cases. We will focus on four such cases: (1) the case in which a class with no methods has attributes, (2) the case in which a class with a single method does not have attributes, (3) the case in which a class with a single method has attribute(s), and (4) the case in which a class with multiple methods does not have attributes. We focus on these four cases because they are the only cases for which one or more of the considered low-level design (LLD) measures have undefined cohesion values. The considered high-level design (HLD) measures have undefined cohesion values for the following four corresponding cases: (1) the case in which a class does not have methods, (2) the case in which a class with a single method does not have parameter types, (3) the case in which a class with a single method has parameter type(s), and (4) the case in which a class with multiple methods does not have parameter types. Table 4.1 lists the measures considered in this study and their values for the aforementioned special cases in terms of the number of methods, attributes, and parameter types. In the table, *m* is the number of methods, and *a* is the number of attributes for LLD measures or the number of distinct parameter types for HLD measures. The table shows that only three measures, namely LSCC, $LCOM_L$, and $LCOM_{HM}$, are defined for all cases. The remaining measures are undefined for most of the cases considered. All the considered measures are defined for the remaining case, which is not included in the table (i.e., the case in which $m>1$ and $a>0$).

4.1.2. Assigning Cohesion Values

When assigning a value for a measure applied on a class that exhibits a special case, two necessary criteria must be considered, as follows.

Criterion 1: Satisfying key cohesion properties. The first criterion is that the assigned value must not cause the measure to violate any of the widely used and accepted cohesion properties proposed by Briand et al. (1998) and explained in Chapter 3. Thus, the assigned values must not cause the measure to be theoretically invalid. Otherwise, the measure becomes ill-defined and its usefulness for indicating cohesion becomes questionable. The only exception to this criterion is when the original definition of the measure violates a property. In this case, the validation of the measure regarding the assigned value can depend on the validation result of the other cases that already have defined values. For example, validating a measure against the *cohesive modules* property requires merging the class under consideration with another class c and comparing the cohesion value of the merged class with each of the cohesion values of the original classes. Therefore, the result of the validation does not depend only on the assigned value but also on the values given by the measure definition for both class c and the merged class, which might have already violated the *cohesive modules* property. Specific examples are later provided for the case in which the original definition of the measure violates the *cohesive modules* property when the values are assigned to $LCOM_H$ (Section 4.1.2.2) and NHD (Section 4.1.2.5). The key cohesion properties must be satisfied by cohesion measures but they are not sufficient to conclude whether the measure is indeed a good cohesion measure.

Table 4.1: Defined and undefined values for the considered measures

Measure	*m*=0 and *a*>0	*m*=1 and *a*=0	*m*=1 and *a*>0	*m*>1 and *a*=0
LSCC	1	1	1	0
$LCOM_{CK1}$, $LCOM_{CK2}$	undefined	undefined	undefined	$m(m-1)/2$
TCC, LCC	undefined	undefined	undefined	0
DC_D, DC_I	undefined	undefined	undefined	α/NP, where α is the number of method pairs that share directly or transitively the invocation of a third method and *NP* is the number of method pairs
CC, SCOM, $LCOM_H$	undefined	undefined	undefined	undefined
$LCOM_L$	0	1	1	*m*
$LCOM_{HM}$	0	1	1	Number of disjoint components considering method invocations
Coh	undefined	undefined	α/a, where α is the summation of the number of distinct attributes accessed by each method in a class.	undefined
CAMC	undefined	undefined	1	undefined
NHD	undefined	undefined	undefined	undefined

Criterion 2: Consistency with common intuition. Common intuition is one way to judge whether a measure indicates cohesion correctly. Therefore, the assigned value must not contradict the common intuition built on (1) the general cohesion definition (i.e., the relatedness among the attributes and methods in a class) and (2) the cohesive interaction

definition as declared by the measure under consideration. As shown in Table 4.1, there are four cases for which certain cohesion measures have undefined values. The first case occurs when a class that has attributes does not have methods. Our interpretation for this case is that we would expect all the attributes to describe the features of the same object. Therefore, the class is expected to be fully cohesive (i.e., the cohesion must be at the maximum and the lack of cohesion must be at the minimum). Conversely, if the attributes are representing unrelated global variables for the whole program, the cohesion of the class must be at the minimum. However, by manual inspection, we found that this case is not featured in any of the classes of the systems considered in this study, which indicates that this case occurs rarely and that, therefore, the assigned cohesion value should not be based on it.

The general definition for a cohesive module (i.e., class in object-oriented software) is that it performs a single task and cannot be easily split. A class that has a single method and no attributes (second case in Table 4.1) is associated with a single task, that is the task performed by its method and cannot be easily split. Therefore, the cohesion value for such a class must be the maximum (the lack of cohesion must be the minimum). However, when the class with a single method has one or more attributes, the intuition becomes dependent on the definition of the cohesive interaction as specified by the measure under consideration. If the cohesive interaction definition is based on the relationships between methods, the cohesion must be the maximum, similar to the previous case, because the class cannot be easily split. However, if the cohesive interaction definition is based on the relationship between the method and the attributes, the cohesion value depends on the (relative) number of attributes referenced by the method. Similarly, if a class with several methods does not have any attributes, the cohesion depends on the cohesive interaction between methods specified by the measure. If the measure considers only the relationships between methods through attributes, the cohesion value must be the minimum, because the methods are unrelated. However, if the measure definition also considers the relationships between methods through method invocations, the cohesion value depends on the (relative) number of methods that are related through invocations. If the measure does not account for relationships through invocations, the methods will be considered unrelated and the cohesion will be the minimum.

We applied these criteria to assign values for the measures under consideration for all the undefined cases. This study does not consider the case in which a class has neither attributes nor methods, because such a class is not frequently declared and used in object-oriented systems.

4.1.2.1. Method-Method Interaction (MMI) Measures

TCC, LCC, DC_D, DC_I, CC, SCOM, $LCOM_{CK1}$, and $LCOM_{CK2}$ are MMI measures because they focus on measuring the interactions between each pair of methods. These measures have the maximum cohesion value of 1 (value of 0 for the lack of cohesion measures $LCOM_{CK1}$ and $LCOM_{CK2}$), and they are undefined for any classes that have fewer than two methods. In addition, CC and SCOM are normalized by dividing the degree of interactions between methods by a factor that depends on the number of attributes. If the class does not have attributes, these measures values are undefined (the cohesion value cannot be infinity). The detailed undefined cases for these measures are shown in the second, third, fourth, and fifth rows in Table 4.1 (the header row is not counted).

A. Cohesion of a Class with No Methods

According to Criterion 2, when the class does not have any methods, the class cohesion value as defined by the MMI measures must be 1. In this case, the assigned value remains in the range of values that do not cause the measures to violate the *non-negativity and normalization* property. In addition, the class has no cohesive interactions, which is at the same time the highest possible number of cohesive interactions. Therefore, the assigned value of 1 does not cause the measures to violate the *null value and maximum value* property. The assigned value does not cause the measures to violate the *monotonicity* property because no cohesive interactions can be added to the class and, therefore, the cohesion cannot be decreased. Finally, the assigned value does not cause the measures to violate the *cohesive modules* property because merging the class under consideration with any other class cannot cause the merged class to assume a cohesion value higher than the class under consideration, because the assigned value of 1 to the class under consideration is the highest possible cohesion value. This discussion demonstrates that the assigned value satisfies Criterion 1. In addition, the assigned value satisfies Criterion 2 because it represents the maximum possible value, as discussed earlier. The same argument applies for both $LCOM_{CK1}$ and $LCOM_{CK2}$ but we recall that these measures measure the lack of cohesion, and therefore, the opposite conclusions (e.g., regarding the maximum and minimum values) are drawn. For example, the lack of cohesion value for the class under consideration is 0. In addition, when the class under consideration is merged with another class C, the lack of cohesion value of the resulting class cannot be less than that for the class under consideration, because the class under consideration exhibits the minimum possible lack of cohesion value.

B. Cohesion of a Class with a Single Method

Based on Criterion 2, when a class has a single method (the second and third cases in Table 4.1), the cohesion value as defined by the MMI measures must be 1 (0 for the lack of cohesion measures). In this case, the assigned value remains within the range of values that do not cause the measures to violate the *non-negativity and normalization* property. Although the class has no cohesive interactions, the class features the maximum possible number of cohesive interactions, which is zero, because the class has a single method and, therefore, that single method has no other methods with which it can interact. As a result, the assigned value does not cause the measures to violate the *null value and maximum value* property. The assigned value does not cause the measures to violate the *monotonicity* property because no cohesive interactions can be added to the class in this case because the class has a single method. Finally, the assigned value does not cause the measures to violate the *cohesive modules* property because merging such a class with any other class cannot cause the merged class to assume a cohesion value higher than the class under consideration, because the class under consideration has the highest possible cohesion value. As a result, the assigned value satisfies Criterion 1, and its assignment is based on Criterion 2.

C. Cohesion of a Class with Multiple Methods and No Attributes

A class with multiple methods and no attributes has defined values for all the considered MMI measures except CC and SCOM. According to Criterion 2, the CC and SCOM values must be 0. As a result, the assigned value remains in the range of values that do not cause the measures to violate the *non-negativity and normalization* property. In addition, the class has no cohesive interactions and, therefore, the assigned value 0 does not cause the measures to violate the *null value and maximum value* property. The assigned value does not cause the measures to violate the *monotonicity* property because the assigned value is the minimum possible value and, therefore, adding a cohesive interaction to the class cannot decrease the cohesion value. When the class under consideration is merged with another class c, the resulting class will have the same number of attributes and similarities between each pair of methods as class c and more methods than in class c. CC and SCOM values are inversely proportional to the number of methods, thus the resulting class will have CC and SCOM values less than those for class c, which verifies that the assigned value does not lead to a violation of the *cohesive modules* property. As a result, the assigned value satisfies Criterion 1 and it is assigned according to Criterion 2.

4.1.2.2. $LCOM_H$

$LCOM_H$ is a lack of cohesion measure and its value ranges within the interval [0, $m/(m-1)$], where m is the number of methods in a class (i.e., the maximum possible lack of cohesion value is 2 when $m = 2$). This measure is originally undefined for all of the four special cases, as shown in Table 4.1, and our proposed values for these cases are as follows.

A. Cohesion of a Class with No Methods

According to Criterion 2, when the class does not have methods, the lack of cohesion value must be the minimum, which is 0. In this case, the assigned value remains in the range of values that do not cause $LCOM_H$ to violate the *non-negativity and normalization* property. In addition, the class cannot have cohesive interactions and, therefore, the assigned value 0 does not cause $LCOM_H$ to violate the *null value and maximum value* property. The assigned value does not cause $LCOM_H$ to violate the *monotonicity* property because no cohesive interactions can be added to the class and, therefore, the cohesion cannot be increased. When the class under consideration is merged with another class, the resulting class cannot have an $LCOM_H$ value less than that for the class under consideration, because the class under consideration has the minimum possible lack of cohesion value. Thus, the *cohesive modules* property is satisfied. As a result, the assigned value does not cause $LCOM_H$ to violate Criterion 1 and it is assigned according to Criterion 2.

B. Cohesion of a Class with a Single Method and No Attributes

Based on Criterion 2, when a class with a single method does not have attributes, its $LCOM_H$ value must be 0 (i.e., the minimum possible lack of cohesion value). Using the same arguments as given in Section 4.1.2.1.B, the assigned value does not cause $LCOM_H$ to violate any of the *non-negativity and normalization*, *null value and maximum value*, or *monotonicity* properties. Finally, the assigned value does not cause $LCOM_H$

to violate the *cohesive modules* property because merging such a class with any other unrelated class cannot cause the merged class to assume a lack of cohesion value that is lower than that of the class under consideration, because the class under consideration has the lowest possible lack of cohesion value. This confirms that the assigned value satisfies Criterion 1. In addition, the assigned value satisfies Criterion 2 as it represents the minimum possible lack of cohesion value, as discussed previously.

C. Cohesion of a Class with a Single Method and One or More Attributes

When a class with a single method has one or more attributes, its $LCOM_H$ value depends on the number of attributes referenced by the method. $LCOM_H$ measures lack of cohesion, it has a maximum value of 2, and it considers the relative number of attributes referenced by the methods. Accordingly, the assigned $LCOM_H$ value in this case is 2×1-α/a), where α is the number of attributes referenced by the method and a is the number of attributes in the class. This value remains in the range of values [0, 2] that do not cause $LCOM_H$ to violate the *non-negativity and normalization* property. In addition, if the class has all possible cohesive interactions, then the lack of cohesion value will be minimum, and if the class does not have any cohesive interactions, then the lack of cohesion value will be maximum. Thus, the assigned value does not cause $LCOM_H$ to violate the *null value and maximum value* property. When a cohesive interaction is added to the class, the $LCOM_H$ value becomes smaller, which does not violate the *monotonicity* property for lack of cohesion measures. $LCOM_H$ already violates the *cohesive modules* property. When the class under consideration is merged with another unrelated class c, to satisfy the *cohesive modules* property, the merged class must have a lack of cohesion value greater than or equal to the lack of cohesion value for class c, which is not always true. For example, if class c has two methods and any number of attributes such that none of the attributes is referenced by the methods, then the $LCOM_H$ value for class c will be 2. If this class is merged with the class under consideration, then the maximum possible $LCOM_H$ value will be 1.5, which causes $LCOM_H$ to violate the *cohesive modules* property. This case is cited as an exception to Criterion 1. Considering the other properties, the assigned value satisfies Criterion 1. In addition, the assigned value satisfies Criterion 2 as it represents the relative number of attributes referenced by the methods of the class.

D. Cohesion of a Class with Multiple Methods and No Attributes

Based on Criterion 2, a class with multiple methods and no attributes must have the maximum possible lack of cohesion value, which is equal to $m/(m-1)$ for $LCOM_H$, where m is the number of methods. In this case, the assigned value remains in the range of values that do not cause $LCOM_H$ to violate the *non-negativity and normalization* property. In addition, the class has no cohesive interactions and, therefore, the assigned value does not cause $LCOM_H$ to violate the *null value and maximum value* property. The assigned value does not cause $LCOM_H$ to violate the *monotonicity* property because the assigned value is the maximum possible lack of cohesion value. Therefore, adding a cohesive interaction to the class cannot increase the lack of cohesion value. The same argument and example, in Section 4.1.2.2.C, regarding the *cohesive modules* property, applies here, indicating that the assigned value cannot satisfy the *cohesive modules* property because $LCOM_H$ itself violates the property. Except for this property, the assigned value satisfies Criterion 1. In addition, the assigned value satisfies Criterion 2 as it represents the maximum possible lack of cohesion value.

4.1.2.3. Coh

Coh accounts for the relative number of attributes referenced by methods, its value ranges within the interval [0, 1], and it is undefined for classes that do not include methods or attributes, as shown in Table 4.1. Our proposed values for these cases are as follows.

A. Cohesion of a Class with No Methods

According to Criterion 2, when the class does not have any methods, the cohesion value must be the maximum, which is 1. Using the same arguments as given in Section 4.1.2.1.A, the assigned value does not cause Coh to violate any of the *non-negativity and normalization, null value and maximum value, monotonicity*, and *cohesive modules* properties and, therefore, Coh satisfies Criterion 1. As a result, the assigned value satisfies Criterion 1 and it is assigned according to Criterion 2.

B. Cohesion of a Class with a Single Method and No Attributes

Based on Criterion 2, when a class with a single method does not have any attributes, its Coh value must be 1 (i.e., the maximum possible cohesion value). This value satisfies Criteria 1 and 2 for the same reasons as discussed above in Section 4.1.2.1.B.

C. Cohesion of a Class with Multiple Methods and No Attributes

According to Criterion 2, a class with multiple methods and no attributes must have the minimum possible cohesion value, which is 0. This value does not cause Coh to violate any of the *non-negativity and normalization, null value and maximum value*, or *monotonicity* properties for the same reasons discussed above in Section 4.1.2.1.C. When the class under consideration is merged with another class c, the resulting class will have more methods than class c and the same number of attributes and number of attributes referenced by methods as class c. The value of Coh is inversely proportional to the number of methods, thus the resulting class will have a Coh value of less than that for class c, which verifies that the assigned value does not lead to a violation of the *cohesive modules* property. As a result, the assigned value satisfies Criterion 1 and it is assigned according to Criterion 2.

4.1.2.4. CAMC

CAMC considers the relative number of distinct types used by the parameters of the methods, its value ranges within the interval [0, 1], and it is undefined for classes that do not include methods or parameters, as shown in Table 4.1. Our proposed values for these cases are as follows.

A. Cohesion of a Class with No Methods

According to Criterion 2, when the class does not have methods, the cohesion value must be the maximum, which is 1. Using the same arguments given in Section 4.1.2.1.A, the assigned value does not cause CAMC to violate any of the *non-negativity and normalization*, *null value and maximum value*, *monotonicity*, or *cohesive modules* properties, and therefore, CAMC satisfies Criterion 1. In addition, the assigned value satisfies Criterion 2 as it represents the maximum possible cohesion value, as discussed earlier.

B. Cohesion of a Class with a Single Method and No Parameters

Based on Criterion 2, when a class has a single method that does not have parameters, its CAMC value must be 1 (i.e., the maximum possible cohesion value). This value satisfies Criteria 1 and 2 for the same reasons as discussed above in Section 4.1.2.1.B.

C. Cohesion of a Class with Multiple Methods and No Parameters

According to Criterion 2, a class with multiple methods, of which none have parameters, must have the minimum possible cohesion value, which is 0. This value does not cause CAMC to violate any of the *non-negativity and normalization*, *null value and maximum value*, or *monotonicity* properties for the same reasons as discussed above in Section 4.1.2.1.C. When the class under consideration is merged with another class c, the resulting class will have the same number of distinct parameter types and number of types of parameters of each method as in class c, and more methods than class c. The value of CAMC is inversely proportional to the number of methods, thus the resulting class will have a CAMC value less than that for class c, which confirms that the assigned value does not lead to a violation in terms of the *cohesive modules* property. As a result, the assigned value satisfies Criterion 1 and it is assigned according to Criterion 2.

4.1.2.5. NHD

NHD is a lack of cohesion measure based on measuring the "agreement", in terms of sharing either the presence or absence of parameter types, between each pair of methods. NHD value ranges within the interval [0, 1], and it is undefined for any classes that have fewer than two methods. In addition, NHD is normalized by dividing the degree of agreements between methods by a factor that depends on the number of parameter types in the class. If none of the methods in the class have parameters, then the measure will be undefined, else the cohesion value will be infinity. Our proposed values for these cases are as follows.

A. Cohesion of a Class with No Methods

According to Criterion 2, when a class does not have methods, the lack of cohesion value using NHD for the class must be 0. Using the same arguments as outlined in Section 4.1.2.2.A, the assigned value does not cause the measure to violate any of the *non-negativity and normalization*, *null value and maximum value*, *monotonicity*, or *cohesive modules* properties. As a result, the assigned value does not violate Criterion 1 and it is assigned according to Criterion 2.

B. Cohesion of a Class with a Single Method

Based on Criterion 2, when a class has a single method with or without parameters, its NHD value must be 0 (i.e., the minimum possible lack of cohesion value). This value satisfies Criteria 1 and 2 for the same reasons as discussed above in Section 4.1.2.1.B.

C. Cohesion of a Class with Multiple Methods and No Parameters

Referring to Criterion 2, a class with multiple methods, of which none have parameters, must have the maximum possible lack of cohesion value, which is 1. This value does not cause NHD to violate any of the *non-negativity and normalization*, *null value and maximum value*, or *monotonicity* properties for the same reasons as discussed above in Section 4.1.2.2.D. Similarly to the discussion in Section 4.1.2.2.C, the assigned value fails to satisfy the *cohesive modules* property because this property depends on the NHD value assigned by the formula of the measure, which already violates the *cohesive modules* property, for other classes that can be merged with the class under consideration. In the context of these other properties, the assigned value satisfies Criterion 1. In addition, the assigned value satisfies Criterion 2 as it represents the maximum possible value for the lack of cohesion, as discussed earlier.

4.1.3. Empirical Validation

This empirical validation explores the applicability of the measures before assigning values to those cases with undefined values, where the applicability of a measure is defined as the percentage of classes for which the measure has defined values. The goal of this study is to determine the percentages of classes that have undefined values in selected systems, thus empirically confirming the importance of this research. In addition, the results of this analysis are used to compare the measures under consideration in terms of their applicability.

We chose four Java open-source software systems from different domains: Art of Illusion v.2.5 (Illusion 2025), GanttProject v.2.0.5 (GanttProject 2025), JabRef v.2.3 beta 2 (JabRef 2025), and Openbravo v.0.0.24 (Openbravo 2025). Art of Illusion consists of 481 classes and about 88 thousand lines of code (KLOC) and is a 3D modeling, rendering, and animation studio system. GanttProject consists of 468 classes and about 39 KLOC, and is a project scheduling application featuring resource management, calendaring, and import/export of several formats (MS Project, HTML, PDF, spreadsheets). JabRef consists of 569 classes and about 48 KLOC and is a graphical application for managing bibliographical databases. Openbravo consists of 447 classes and about 36 KLOC and is a point-of-sale application designed for touchscreens. We chose these four open-source systems from http://sourceforge.net. The restrictions taken into account in choosing these systems were that they (1) are implemented using Java, (2) are relatively medium in terms of the number of classes, (3) are from different domains, and (4) have available source code and fault repositories.

Considering all classes in the four selected systems, Table 4.2 shows the numbers and percentages of classes that have undefined cohesion values. The first and second rows report the name and numbers of classes for each system. The third row reports the numbers and percentages of special classes (i.e., those classes that have undefined cohesion values when applying one or more of the considered measures) in each system. The remaining rows include the numbers and percentages of classes that feature each of the special cases (i.e., cases in which a class has an undefined cohesion value using at least one of the considered measures) for each system. The percentages in these rows are calculated in terms of the ratio of the number of classes featuring the special case to the number of classes in the system. In the first column, c_i, m, a, and p are the special case identifier and the number of methods, attributes, and distinct parameter types, respectively. The last column summarizes the results across all systems. The number of special classes in each system, reported in the third row, is not equal to the sum of the number of classes across the preceding rows, because the classes in the last three rows overlap with the classes considered in the preceding three rows. For example, if a class with a method that has parameters (case c_7) also includes attributes, it will also be considered in the sixth row (case c_3).

Table 4.2: The numbers and percentages of special classes and cases

	Illusion	Gantt	JabRef	Openbravo	All Systems
No. of classes	481	468	569	447	1,965
No. of special classes	87 (18.1%)	136 (29.1%)	273 (48%)	132 (29.5%)	628 (32%)
c_1: m=0 and a>0	5 (1%)	8 (1.7%)	0 (0%)	1 (0.2%)	14 (0.7%)
c_2: m=1 and a=0	10 (2.1%)	42 (9%)	108 (19%)	25 (5.6%)	185 (9.4%)
c_3: m=1 and a>0	24 (5%)	11 (2.4%)	25 (4.4%)	12 (2.7%)	72 (3.7%)
c_4: m>1 and a=0	45 (9.4%)	72 (15.4%)	135 (23.7%)	86 (19.2%)	338 (17.2%)
c_5: m=1 and p=0	10 (2.1%)	13 (2.8%)	41 (7.2%)	7 (1.6%)	71 (3.6%)
c_6: m>1 and p=0	4 (0.8%)	20 (4.3%)	21 (3.7%)	20 (4.5%)	65 (3.3%)
c_7: m=1 and p>0	24 (5%)	40 (8.5%)	92 (16.2%)	30 (6.7%)	186 (9.5%)

The results in Table 4.2 suggest that the percentages of classes that feature special cases are relatively high (ranging from 18% to 48%). Across all systems, 32% of the classes are special. When an empirical study is performed to explore the correlations between measures and to compare, in an unbiased manner, the measures in terms of their ability to precisely indicate class quality, classes with undefined cohesion values according to any of the considered measures are removed. This class removal leads to two problems. The first is that decreasing the number of classes included in the empirical study can decrease the accuracy of the results. The second is that removing special classes that feature widely used cases can limit the representation of the results and can lead to incorrect conclusions in deciding which measures are better at predicting cohesion.

We consider the fifteen cohesion measures listed in Table 4.1, and we define the applicability of a measure in terms of the percentage of classes for which the measure has defined cohesion values. We recall that one of the major goals of the study is to increase the applicability of each measure to 100% by assigning values for all of the undefined cases, as illustrated in Section 4.1.2. For each measure, Table 4.3 reports the number of classes for which the measure is applicable and the applicability of the measure (in parentheses) using the classes in each system and across all of the systems together (last column). Those measures that have the same special cases, i.e., for which the measures have undefined values as shown in Table 4.1, are grouped together. The second column lists those cases for which the measures have undefined values and the listed cases can be used to map Table 4.3 to Table 4.2. For example, Table 4.3 shows that Coh is undefined for cases c_1, c_2, and c_4. From Table 4.2, we see that 5, 10, and 45 classes in the Illusion system feature cases c_1, c_2, and c_4, respectively. Thus, the total number of special classes is 5+10+45 = 60, and the total number of classes for which Coh is applicable equals 481- 60 = 421, which is reported in the third row for the Illusion system in Table 4.3. The applicability in this case is 421/481 = 87.5%. Similarly, the results in the other columns of Table 4.3 are obtained. For the measures that have undefined values for some cases, CAMC has the highest applicability (89.1% – 96%) and $LCOM_H$, CC, and SCOM have the lowest applicabilities (52.9% – 82.5%) across all systems.

4.1.4. Summary

The assigned measure values for the four special cases under consideration are summarized in Table 4.4. All these values satisfy both Criteria 1 and 2, with the exceptions stated for Criterion 1. These assigned values allow the measures to be applicable for any class.

Table 4.3: Applicability of the considered measures

Measure	Non-applicable (special) cases	Illusion	Gantt	JabRef	Open bravo	All Systems
LSCC, $LCOM_L$, $LCOM_{HM}$	-	481 (100%)	468 (100%)	569 (100%)	447 (100%)	1965 (100%)
Coh	c_1, c_2, c_4	421 (87.5%)	346 (73.9%)	326 (57.3%)	335 (74.9%)	1428 (72.7%)
TCC, LCC, DC_D, DC_I, $LCOM_{CK1}$, $LCOM_{CK2}$	c_1, c_2, c_3	442 (91.9%)	407 (87%)	436 (76.6%)	409 (91.5%)	1694 (86.2%)
$LCOM_H$, CC, SCOM	c_1, c_2, c_3, c_4	397 (82.5%)	335 (71.6%)	301 (52.9%)	323 (72.3%)	1356 (69%)
CAMC	c_1, c_5, c_6	462 (96%)	427 (91.2%)	507 (89.1%)	419 (93.7%)	1815 (92.4%)
NHD	c_1, c_5, c_6, c_7	438 (91.1%)	387 (82.7%)	415 (72.9%)	389 (87%)	1629 (82.9%)

Table 4.4: The assigned values for the measures under consideration

Measure	***m*=0 and *a*>0**	***m*=1 and *a*=0**	***m*=1 and *a*>0**	***m*>1 and *a*=0**
TCC, LCC, CC, SCOM, CAMC	1	1	1	0
DC_D, DC_I	1	1	1	Assigned before
$LCOM_{CK1}$, $LCOM_{CK2}$	0	0	0	Assigned before
$LCOM_H$	0	0	2*(1-α/*a*), where α is the summation of the number of distinct attributes accessed by each method in a class.	m/(m-1)
Coh	1	1	Assigned before	0
NHD	0	0	0	1

4.2. Accounting for Data Encapsulation in Cohesion Measurement

4.2.1. Motivation

Object-oriented (OO) programming enforces modularity through using an encapsulation feature, which refers to bundling data (i.e., values of a set of attributes) and methods that operate on that data together within an object. In an OO program, an object can implicitly refer to several attributes. Creating an object implies invoking the object's constructor method, which typically initializes the object's attributes. An attribute in an object-oriented program can be of either a primitive or a reference type. Primitive types are elementary types that are supported by an OO programming language (e.g., int, float, double, short, and boolean in Java), whereas a reference type can be either an array or an object. Consequently, a primitive type always refers to a single data element, whereas due to the encapsulation feature, a reference type can refer to multiple data elements.

Some cohesion measures (e.g., $LCOM_{CK1}$, $LCOM_{CK2}$, $LCOM_{L}$, $LCOM_{HM}$, TCC, LCC) consider a pair of methods to be cohesive when they share a common attribute regardless of the number of shared attributes. In this case, counterintuitively, two pairs of methods are considered to have the same cohesion degree even when one pair share a single attribute and the other pair share all of the attributes in the class. This problem was solved by accounting for the number of distinct attributes referenced by each method in the class (e.g., $LCOM_{H}$ and Coh) or by considering the number of distinct shared attributes between each pair of methods in the class (e.g., LSCC, CC, and SCOM). These measures are based on the intuition that the cohesion level increases as the number of referenced attributes or the number of attributes that are shared between methods increases, and vice versa. However, these measures do not consider the fact that the referenced or shared attributes can be of different types that belong to different categories (namely, primitive or reference). In other words, as per our knowledge, none of the existing class cohesion measures consider the fact that the reference of an attribute of an object type is potentially a reference to several encapsulated attributes. Therefore, intuitively, a pair of methods (PMs) that share a common attribute of an object type is potentially more cohesive than a PMs that share a common primitive attribute. In addition, a PMs that share a common attribute of an object type that encapsulates more attributes is intuitively more cohesive than those that encapsulate fewer attributes. The same concept of giving higher cohesion weights to object types compared with primitive types or to object types that encapsulate a smaller number of attributes must be applied when considering the class cohesion measures that account for the types of method parameters (e.g., CAMC and NHD).

In this section, we list an algorithm for assigning weights to attributes and parameters. The weight of an attribute or a parameter of an object type depends on the number of the object type's encapsulated attributes. Both direct and transitive data encapsulation (DE) are addressed, where a transitive DE occurs when an attribute is an object of a class that has some attributes of object types. In addition, we account for inheritance in the proposed attribute/parameter weight assignment algorithm. That is, the number of encapsulated attributes of an object of a class *c* depends on the number of attributes defined in or inherited by class *c*. We extend seven existing class cohesion measures to consider the weights of the attributes in cohesion measurement. These measures are the ones that are based on counting the number of accessed or shared attributes or parameter types. Other measures are not considered either because they are not precise enough to distinguish between accessing/sharing a single attribute and accessing/sharing multiple attributes or because they are based on an entirely different measurement approach, such as the approach of using graph theory concepts.

4.2.2. Attribute/Parameter Weight Assignment Algorithm

Class cohesion measures do not account for the size of the attributes (e.g., in terms of the number of bytes); instead, some of them account for the number of attributes that are referenced or shared by the methods in a class. Therefore, each attribute of a primitive type is assigned to a weight of value "1" regardless of its size. Conversely, we propose the weight assignment recursive algorithm given in Figure 4.1 to assign weights to the attributes of the object types. Before measuring the cohesion of a class a weight has to be assigned to each attribute of an object type. Therefore, the algorithm given in Figure 4.1 has to be applied to each attribute of an object type *c*, in the class. The algorithm takes class *c* (i.e., the object type) as an input parameter, it marks all of the classes in the system as *unvisited*, and it starts computing the weight of class *c* by calling the recursive procedure *weight*. The *weight* procedure starts by assigning an initial weight of "1" to class *c* to represent the class's object itself, regardless of its encapsulated attributes. This assignment avoids incorrectly assigning an attribute with no encapsulated data a weight of zero because, in this case, a pair of methods that share this object will be incorrectly considered to be unrelated unless they share some other attributes.

In OO programming, it is allowable to have a cyclic reference. That is, class *c* is allowed to include an attribute of type *c*. In addition, the class is allowed to include an attribute of class *b* that encapsulates an attribute of class *c*. This cyclic reference causes an object attribute to have an infinite weight. To avoid this scenario, the algorithm breaks the infinite loop by checking whether the traversed class was already visited. If the answer is yes, then the weight of the object will be equal to the number of attributes that are defined and inherited by class *c* (in addition to the initial weight "1"). Otherwise, the algorithm marks the class as visited (to avoid future infinite recursion calls of an algorithm) and increases the weight of the class by a value that is equal to the number of attributes encapsulated in the class regardless of whether these attributes are defined in or inherited by class *c*. In its turn, an encapsulated attribute can be of a primitive or an object type. An attribute of a primitive type causes the weight of class *c* to be increased by "1", whereas an attribute of an object type causes the weight of the class to be increased by the weight of its type, which is computed by recursively invoking the *weight* procedure.

```
Algorithm: Weight assignment algorithm
Input: Class c, which is the type of an object attribute
Output: Weight of the object attribute
Postcondition: Weight of the object attribute is an integer value
               greater than or equal to 1.
Steps:
compute_weight(class c) {
    Mark all classes as unvisited
    return weight(c)
}

weight(class s) {
    w=1
    if class s is marked as visited, then
          w = w + number of attributes defined and inherited by
class s
    else
          mark class s as visited
          for each attribute of type t in class s
               if t is primitive, then w = w + 1
               else w = w + weight( t )
          for each class/interface e extended/implemented by class s
               for each attribute of type t in class/interface e
                       if t is primitive, then w = w + 1
                       else w = w + weight( t )
```

Figure 4.1: Weight assignment algorithm for an object attribute of type *c*.

Figure 4.2 shows sample Java code for three classes, *Circle*, *Cylinder*, and *Draw*. The *Draw* class has three methods, an attribute of a primitive type, and two object attributes. The *Cylinder* class defines an attribute of a primitive type and inherits the *Circle* class, which has an attribute of a primitive type. Each of the *radius*, *height*, and *id* attributes is assigned a weight of "1" because these attributes are of primitive types. When the algorithm in Figure 4.1 is applied to find the weight for the attribute *cd* in the class *Draw*, the weight is initialized to "1". The weight is then increased by two because the class *Cylinder* defines an attribute of weight "1" and inherits an attribute of weight "1". This application results in assigning the attribute *cd* a weight of "3". Similarly, the application of the algorithm results in assigning a weight of "2" to attribute *c* in class *Draw*. Figure 4.2 also provides the attribute/method and parameter-type/method reference matrices, where a value of "1" in row *i* and column *j* indicates that the attribute/parameter-type *j* is referenced by method *i*. Otherwise, the value is set to "0".

4.2.3. Extended Class Cohesion Measures

The considered cohesion measures are extended to consider the weights of the attributes/parameter-types. The resulting formulas are listed in Table 4.5. The extension considers the fact that a column *c* with a weight *w* in a DMA or a DPT matrix can be re-represented by a set of *w* columns; each of them is identical to column *c* but has a weight of "1". For example, the Coh measure considers the average number of "1"s in a DMA matrix. When a column in a DMA matrix has a weight of "2", a cell in this column with a value of "1" is considered as though it is two cells such that each of them has a value of "1". This consideration of the weight results in counting this value of "1" as $(2 \times 1 = 2)$. Therefore, the formula of the Coh measure is extended by multiplying the value of each cell in a column by the weight of the column. In addition, the value *n*, which represents the number of attributes is substituted by the summation of the weights of the attributes. This substitution is performed due to the fact that when a column in a DMA matrix has a weight of "2", it is considered as though it is two columns such that each of them has a weight of "1". The same concept applies for all of the considered measures.

```
class Circle {
        double radius;
        ...
}
class Cylinder extends Circle{
        double height;
        ....
}
public class Draw{
        Circle c;
        Cylinder cd;
        int id;
        void circle_declaration(Circle cr){
                c=cr;
                id=0;
        }
        void cylinder_declaration
                        (Cylinder cy){
                cd=cy;
                id=1;
        }
        void print_current_shape(){
                if (id==0)
            System.out.println("circle");
                else
          System.out.println("cylinder");
        }
}
```

Weight	2	3	1
	c	cd	id
circle_declaration	1	0	1
cylinder_declaration	0	1	1
print_current_shape	0	0	1

Direct Method-Attribute (DMA) matrix

Weight	2	3
	Circle	Cylinder
Circle_declaration	1	0
cylinder_declaration	0	1
print_current_shape	0	0

Direct Parameter-Type (DPT) matrix

Figure 4.2: Sample partial Java code and its corresponding attribute/method and parameter-type/method reference matrices

It is important to note that the formulas of the similarity between a pair of methods in LSCC, CC, and SCOM are extended by considering the weights of the columns in a DMA matrix, but the general definition of the measures (i.e., the cohesion is computed as the average of the similarities of the method pairs) is not affected by the extension, and therefore, the original definition is not modified. Consequently, Table 4.5 lists the modified formula of the similarity for each of LSCC, CC, and SCOM. The general formula is the same as the formula given in Chapter 2. For each of the considered measures, we applied each of the original and modified formulas to obtain the corresponding cohesion values of the *Draw* class given in Figure 4.2, and we report the results in Table 4.5.

The results in Table 4.5 show that the consideration of the encapsulated data within the attributes/parameters of object types can alter the obtained cohesion values. The values obtained using the modified formulas better represent the class cohesion level because those values account for the encapsulation feature in OO programming.

4.2.4. Empirical Analysis for the Cohesion Values

This section reports and discusses an empirical study that investigates the impact of considering the weights of the attributes and parameter types due to the DE feature in cohesion measurement. The empirical study has the following specific goals:

1. Goal *G4.1*: The first goal is to explore whether it is worthwhile to study the impact of the DE feature in cohesion measurement. This goal is achieved by obtaining the percentage of attributes and methods parameters of object types in the classes. A high percentage of these attributes and parameters in the classes gives an indication that it is worthwhile to address the problem of DE consideration in cohesion measurement.

2. Goal *G4.2*: The second goal is to investigate the trends in the changes in cohesion values that are obtained using the modified formulas of cohesion measures when the attributes and parameters of the object types are assigned weights that are different from those of the primitive types. We achieved this goal by obtaining the mean cohesion values of the

classes at different constant weights (from 1 to 10) that are assigned to attributes and parameters of object types and visualizing the results.

Table 4.5: Formulas of the extended cohesion measures and the corresponding *Draw* class cohesion values.

Measure	Modified Formula	*Draw* cohesion value using the original formula	*Draw* cohesion value using the modified formula
$LCOM_H$	$\frac{\sum_{i=1}^{m}\sum_{j=1}^{n} c_{ij}\times w_j - m\times\sum_{j=1}^{n} w_j}{(1-m)\times\sum_{j=1}^{n} w_j}$	0.667	0.833
Coh	$\frac{\sum_{i=1}^{m}\sum_{j=1}^{n} c_{ij}\times w_j}{m\times\sum_{j=1}^{n} w_j}$	0.555	0.444
$S(m_i,m_k)$ in LSCC	$\frac{\sum_{j=1}^{n} c_{ij}\times c_{kj}\times w_j}{\sum_{j=1}^{n} w_j}$	0.333	0.167
$S(m_i,m_k)$ in CC	$\frac{\sum_{j=1}^{n} c_{ij}\times c_{kj}\times w_j}{\sum_{j=1}^{n} (c_{ij}\vee c_{kj})\times w_j}$	0.444	0.25
$S(m_i,m_k)$ in SCOM	$\frac{\sum_{j=1}^{n} (c_{ij}\times c_{kj}\times w_j)\times\sum_{j=1}^{n} (c_{ij}\vee c_{kj})\times w_j}{\sum_{j=1}^{n} w_j\times\min(\sum_{j=1}^{n}(c_{ij}\times w_j),\sum_{j=1}^{n}(c_{kj}\times w_j))}$	0.611	0.5
CAMC	$\frac{m+\sum_{i=1}^{m}\sum_{j=1}^{n} c_{ij}\times w_j}{m\times(\sum_{j=1}^{n} w_j+1)}$	0.556	0.444
NHD	$1-\frac{2}{m\times\sum_{j=1}^{n} w_j\times(m-1)}\times\sum_{j=1}^{n}(w_j\times\sum_{i=1}^{m} c_{ij}\times(m-\sum_{i=1}^{m} c_{ij}))$	0.333	0.333

3. Goal *G4.3*: The third goal of this empirical study is to explore whether the consideration of the weights assigned by the algorithm given in Figure 4.1 causes the cohesion values obtained using the selected measures to significantly change. This goal is achieved by applying the proposed weight assignment algorithm on the attributes and parameters in the selected classes and obtaining the corresponding cohesion values using the considered cohesion measures. These values are statistically compared to the values obtained using the original cohesion measures. The corresponding null hypothesis is as follows:

   Null Hypothesis 1: Considering DE in cohesion measurement does not cause the cohesion values obtained using the considered measures to significantly change.

4. Goal *G4.4*. The fourth goal of this empirical study is to explore whether, instead of applying the weight assignment algorithm, there is a constant weight that can be assigned to the attributes and parameters of object types such that the resulting cohesion values are not significantly different from those obtained when the algorithm is considered. This goal is achieved by trying out several constant weights and statistically comparing the corresponding cohesion values with those obtained when the algorithm is applied. There are two key differences between this process and the one indicated for *Goal G4.2*. First, this process considers constant weights that can be greater than 10, whereas the process required for *Goal G4.2* considers only constant weights between 1 and 10. The second difference is that this process statistically tests whether the cohesion values obtained at different constant weights are significantly different than each other, whereas such a test is not considered in *Goal G4.2*. The corresponding null hypothesis is as follows:

   Null Hypothesis 2: Given a specific cohesion measure, there exists a constant weight that can be assigned to the attributes and parameters of object types such that this constant weight can yield cohesion measurement values not significantly different from those obtained using the weight assignment algorithm.

In this empirical study, we consider the seven cohesion measures and their extensions, as listed in Table 4.5. As explained in Section 4.2.1, these measures are selected because their definitions consider the number of distinct attributes or parameter types that are accessed by the methods in a class or they account for the similarity degree between pairs of methods. Therefore, the application of these measures is affected by the consideration of the weights of the attributes or parameter types. The empirical study involves classes in five systems. The descriptions of these systems, the studies, and their results are given as follows.

4.2.4.1. Software Systems

We selected five Java open-systems as described in Table 4.6. The systems have variety of sizes in terms of the number of classes and the number of lines of code. Except for JHotDraw, each of the considered systems falls within the large-size-system category (i.e., the number of classes is greater than 1000). Only JHotDraw is a medium-sized system. The source and binary codes are available for all of these systems, which allowed us to apply our cohesion measurement tool on them.

We implemented a tool that takes as an input the binary files of the classes in a system and a set of constant weights to be considered. The tool creates a text file that contains the outputs and can be opened and manipulated using Excel. For each class in the considered system, the output file includes the class (1) name and package, (2) the total number of attributes and distinct parameter types, (3) the number of attributes and distinct parameters of object types, (4) the cohesion values that are obtained using the original definitions of the seven considered measures, (5) the cohesion measures that are obtained using the extended measures when considering the constant weights entered by the user, and (6) the cohesion values that are obtained using the extended measures when considering the weights obtained according to the algorithm given in Figure 4.1.

Table 4.6: Descriptions of the considered systems

System	Version	Date of release	Domain	No. of classes	LOC
Eclipse (Eclipse 2025)	1.0.1	August 8, 2008	Multi-language software development environment	5753	789 K
DrJava (DrJava 2025)	beta-2009 0505-r4932	May 5, 2009	A lightweight programming environment for Java designed to foster test-driven software development.	1463	204 K
Art Of Illusion (Art Of Illusion 2025)	2.5.1	October 22, 2007	3D modeling, rendering, and animation studio system	1435	321 K
FreeMind (FreeMind 2025)	0.8.1	February 26, 2008	Hierarchical editing system	1230	170 K
JHotDraw (JHotDraw 2025)	7.4.1	January 17, 2010	Java graphics framework for structured drawing editors	846	107 K

We applied the tool to all of the classes in the considered systems. We used the results to obtain the percentage of the attributes and parameters of object types in each of the five systems, and we visualized the results in the chart given in Figure 4.2. The results demonstrate that the percentage of attributes of object types ranges between 45% and 77%, with an average of 67.7%. The percentage of the parameters of object types ranges from 87% to 89%, with an average of 84.8%. Generally, the results indicate that a relatively high percentage of attributes/parameters are of object types. Therefore, this analysis achieves the goal *G4.1* and it indicates that it is worthwhile to study the impact of the consideration of DE in cohesion measurement.

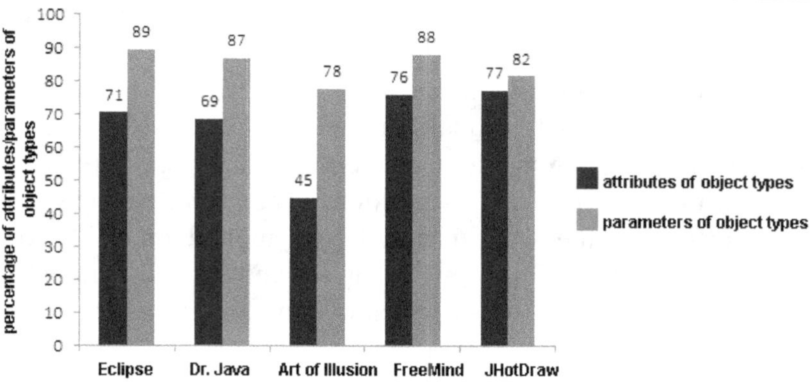

Figure 4.2: Percentage of attributes/parameters of object types

4.2.4.2. Analysis of Cohesion Value Changes

To achieve goal *G4.2*, we applied a tool to obtain the cohesion values for weights from 1 to 10. For example, when a weight is assigned to 5, then all of the weights of the attributes and parameters of object types are set to 5 instead of applying the weight assignment algorithm given in Figure 4.1, and the extended measures are applied. This weight assignment allows us to explore how the cohesion values obtained using the considered cohesion measures change as the weights of the attributes/parameters of object types change. It is important to note that assigning a weight of 1 to the attributes/parameters of object types and applying the extended measures is identical to ignoring the weights and applying the original formulas of the measures because, in this case, the attributes/parameters of object and primitive types have the same weight of "1". We obtained the mean value of the cohesion values at each weight for each measure when applied on classes in each system. We visualized the results using the charts in Figure 4.3.

We tested the significance of the difference between the original cohesion values (i.e., when the weight is assigned to 1) and the values when the weight is assigned to 10. For the classes of each of the considered systems, we applied the Shapiro-Wilk normality test (Rosenkrantz 2008) to check whether the cohesion values follow the normal distribution (i.e., the test was applied on 2 weights × 7 measures × 5 systems = 70 data sets). The size of a data set is equal to the number of classes included in a considered system. None of the tested data sets were found to follow the normal distribution. Therefore, to test the significance of the value changes, we applied the Wilcoxon paired test (Devore 2011), which is a standard non-parametric statistical technique that is applied to compare two independent sets of samples that are not necessarily normal. A pair of data sets are considered significantly different when the obtained p-value is greater than the typical significance threshold ($\alpha = 0.05$). The test is applied to test the significance of the difference between the pairs of cohesion values obtained when the weight is assigned to 1 and those obtained when the weight is assigned to 10, for each measure applied to classes of each systems (i.e., the test was applied on: 7 measures × 5 systems = 35 pairs of data sets). Table 4.7 reports the obtained p-values

The results shown in Figure 4.3 and Table 4.7 lead to the following observations:

- **Direction of change**: The results indicate that the direction of change in the cohesion values when the different weights are considered differ from one measure to another. The results show that the mean values obtained using Coh, LSCC, CC, and SCOM increase as the weights of the attributes of object types increase. Inversely, the mean values obtained using $LCOM_H$ decrease as the weights of the attributes of object types increase. Because $LCOM_H$ measures the absence of cohesion, the results of the first five measures indicate that the class cohesion increases as the weights of the attributes of object types increase. The results also show that there is a negative relationship between the mean CAMC value and the weight of the parameter types. Finally, the results demonstrated that the direction of change in the NHD mean values differed from one system to another (i.e., the mean NHD value decreased for the classes of Eclipse and DrJava and increased for the classes of the other three systems as the weight of the parameters of object types increased).

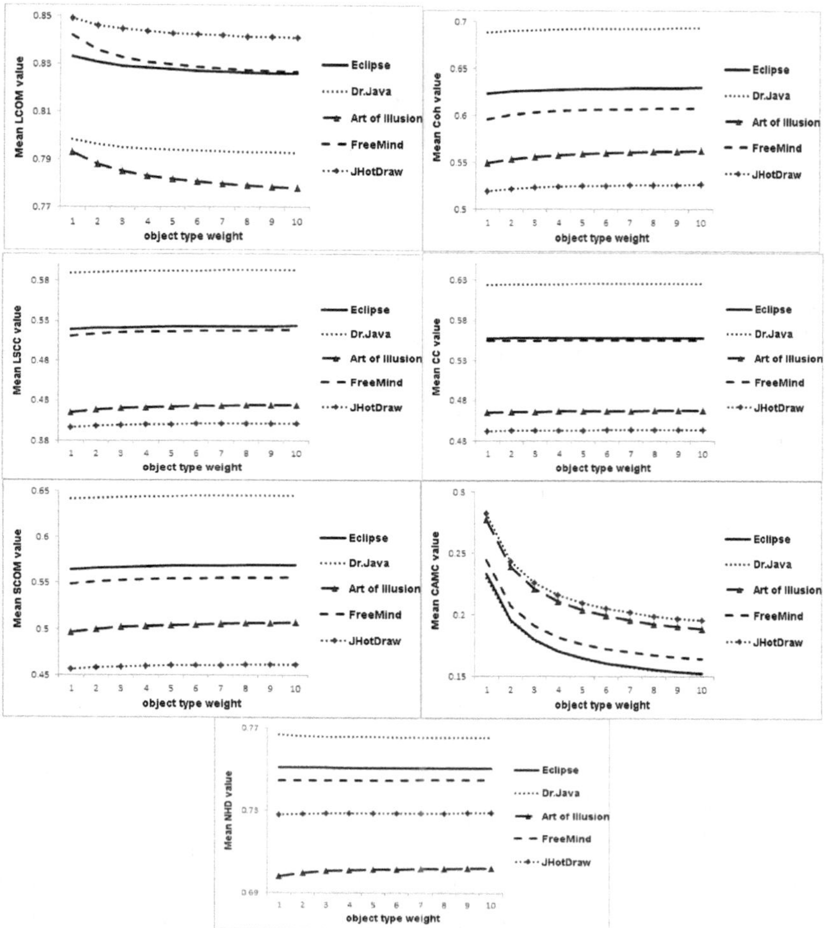

Figure 4.3: The change in the mean cohesion values as the weights of the attributes/parameters of object types change.

- **Amount and significance of change**: The amount of change caused by the consideration of the weights of the attributes of object types differs from one measure to another and from one system to another. The greatest changes occurred when $LCOM_H$ was considered, and the smallest changes appeared when CC was considered. When the weights of the parameters of object types were considered, the mean values of NHD changed slightly, whereas the mean values of CAMC changed considerably. With few exceptions featured for NHD values obtained for classes in two systems, Wilcoxon paired test results show that the values obtained at weight 10 are significantly different than the original cohesion values.

Table 4.7: Wilcoxon p-value values for the considered pairs of scenarios (considering weight of "10" comparing to weight of "1".

System/ measure	$LCOM_H$	Coh	LSCC	CC	SCOM	CAMC	NHD
Eclipse	< 0.0001	< 0.0001	< 0.0001	< 0.0001	< 0.0001	< 0.0001	< 0.0001
DrJava	0.0001	0.0001	< 0.0001	< 0.0001	< 0.0001	< 0.0001	0.0012
Art of Illusion	< 0.0001	< 0.0001	< 0.0001	0.0004	< 0.0001	< 0.0001	< 0.0001
FreeMind	< 0.0001	< 0.0001	< 0.0001	0.0134	0.0001	< 0.0001	0.6473
JHotDraw	< 0.0001	< 0.0001	< 0.0001	< 0.0001	< 0.0001	< 0.0001	0.5361

This section showed how the cohesion values change as the considered weights change; therefore, the cohesion values obtained when the algorithm in Figure 4.1 was applied were not considered. The next section considers the significance of the change compared to the cohesion values obtained when the algorithm given in Figure 4.1 was applied.

4.2.4.3. Analysis of the Significance of Change in the Cohesion Values

To achieve goal *G4.3* and accept or reject *Null Hypothesis 1*, we considered the tool outputs regarding the cohesion values in the case in which the algorithm given in Figure 4.1 was applied to assign weights to attributes and parameters of object types. The considered systems use two types of libraries: the Java Development Kit (JDK) library and other open-source libraries. The source and binary codes of the JDK are not available within the downloadable part of the system, whereas the source and binary codes of the other used libraries are downloadable. Therefore, it was infeasible to apply our algorithm to obtain the weights of objects of JDK classes such as *String*. For such objects, we set the weight to "2" because this value is the smallest value that differentiates attributes of object types from those of primitive types. Other than this approximation, we applied the proposed algorithm as is. Table 4.8 lists the descriptive statistics of the cohesion values obtained using the original definitions of the measures (i.e., the weight w_1 is set to "1") and the proposed extended formulas of the measures (i.e., the weight w_2 differs from one object to another and is assigned according to the algorithm given in Figure 4.1) when these measures were applied on Eclipse classes. The descriptive statistics of the remaining considered systems are provided in Tables 4.9 – 4.12.

Table 4.8: Descriptive statistics for the considered measures applied on Eclipse.

Measure	Weight	Min	Max	25%	Med	75%	Mean	Std. Dev.
$LCOM_H$	w_1	0	2	0.50	0.85	1.14	0.83	0.51
	w_2	0	2	0.50	0.82	1.14	0.82	0.52
Coh	w_1	0	1	0.28	0.67	1.00	0.62	0.37
	w_2	0	1	0.31	0.67	1.00	0.64	0.36
LSCC	w_1	0	1	0.07	0.38	1.00	0.52	0.43
	w_2	0	1	0.08	0.42	1.00	0.53	0.43
CC	w_1	0	1	0.15	0.49	1.00	0.56	0.41
	w_2	0	1	0.15	0.50	1.00	0.56	0.41
SCOM	w_1	0	1	0.14	0.53	1.00	0.56	0.41
	w_2	0	1	0.16	0.58	1.00	0.57	0.41
CAMC	w_1	0	1	0.00	0.21	0.40	0.23	0.24
	w_2	0	1	0.00	0.08	0.27	0.17	0.21
	$w_3 = 5$	0	1	0.00	0.12	0.27	0.16	0.19
NHD	w_1	0	1	0.61	0.81	1.00	0.75	0.28
	w_2	0	1	0.60	0.84	1.00	0.76	0.28

Table 4.9: Descriptive statistics for the considered measures applied to DrJava.

Measure	Weight	Min	Max	25%	Med	75%	Mean	Std. Dev.
$LCOM_H$	w_1	0	2	0.43	0.83	1.14	0.80	0.52
	w_2	0	2	0.40	0.80	1.14	0.79	0.52
Coh	w_1	0	1	0.38	0.81	1.00	0.69	0.34
	w_2	0	1	0.40	0.83	1.00	0.70	0.33
LSCC	w_1	0	1	0.14	0.64	1.00	0.59	0.42
	w_2	0	1	0.16	0.68	1.00	0.60	0.41
CC	w_1	0	1	0.23	0.71	1.00	0.62	0.39
	w_2	0	1	0.24	0.71	1.00	0.63	0.39
	$w_3 = 5$	0	1	0.24	0.71	1.00	0.63	0.39
SCOM	w_1	0	1	0.26	0.86	1.00	0.64	0.39
	w_2	0	1	0.28	0.87	1.00	0.65	0.39
CAMC	w_1	0	1	0.00	0.21	0.40	0.23	0.23
	w_2	0	1	0.00	0.12	0.33	0.18	0.20
NHD	w_1	0	1	0.62	0.80	1.00	0.77	0.26
	w_2	0	1	0.60	0.81	1.00	0.77	0.26
	$w_3 = 1$	0	1	0.62	0.80	1.00	0.77	0.26

Our goal here is to test whether the cohesion values obtained at w_1 and w_2 are significantly different. We applied the Wilcoxon paired test to check the significance of the difference between the pairs of cohesion values obtained at w_1 and w_2 for each measure applied to classes of each systems (i.e., the test was applied on: 7 measures × 5 systems = 35 pairs of data sets, where the size of a data set is equal to the number of classes included in a considered system). The Wilcoxon technique was applied because according to the Shapiro-Wilk normality test, none of the data sets were found to follow the normal distribution.

We have found that 91.4% of the considered pairs are significantly different. Only three pairs (i.e., the pairs of data obtained using NHD when applied on the classes of each of DrJava and JHotDraw systems and the pair of data obtained using CC when applied on FreeMind classes) were not found to be significantly different. Therefore, we rejected *Null Hypothesis 1* and concluded that the consideration of DE in cohesion measurement can cause the cohesion values obtained using the considered measures to significantly change.

Table 4.10: Descriptive statistics for the considered measures applied to Art of Illusion.

Measure	Weight	Min	Max	25%	Med	75%	Mean	Std. Dev.
$LCOM_H$	w_1	0	2	0.53	0.79	1.00	0.79	0.50
	w_2	0	2	0.50	0.75	1.00	0.77	0.51
	$w_3 = 47$	0	2	0.50	0.77	0.99	0.77	0.51
Coh	w_1	0	1	0.25	0.49	1.00	0.55	0.34
	w_2	0	1	0.28	0.50	1.00	0.57	0.34
	$w_3 = 55$	0	1	0.26	0.50	1.00	0.57	0.34
LSCC	w_1	0	1	0.06	0.20	1.00	0.42	0.41
	w_2	0	1	0.07	0.24	1.00	0.43	0.41
	$w_3 = 24$	0	1	0.06	0.22	1.00	0.43	0.41
CC	w_1	0	1	0.12	0.31	1.00	0.47	0.39
	w_2	0	1	0.13	0.31	1.00	0.47	0.39
SCOM	w_1	0	1	0.13	0.40	1.00	0.50	0.39
	w_2	0	1	0.15	0.43	1.00	0.51	0.38
	$w_3 = 57$	0	1	0.14	0.42	1.00	0.51	0.39
CAMC	w_1	0	1	0.00	0.27	0.43	0.28	0.23
	w_2	0	1	0.00	0.15	0.33	0.20	0.21
	$w_3 = 5$	0	1	0.00	0.17	0.31	0.20	0.20
NHD	w_1	0	1	0.56	0.75	0.90	0.70	0.27
	w_2	0	1	0.55	0.76	0.92	0.70	0.28
	$w_3 = 7$	0	1	0.56	0.76	0.91	0.70	0.27

The weight assignment algorithm is a recursive algorithm, and therefore, its manual application can be difficult in some cases. Thus, we investigated whether there is a constant weight that consistently leads to cohesion values that are not significantly different compared with those obtained when using the algorithm to assign the weights. Section 4.2.4.4 reports a study that investigates this interesting problem.

4.2.4.4. Consideration of Constant Weights

To achieve goal *G4.4* and accept or reject *Null Hypothesis 2*, for each measure and for the classes in each system, we used our tool to obtain the cohesion values at specific weights. We started by setting w_f=1. We used the Wilcoxon test to compare the obtained values with the values when w is set to w_2 (i.e., the values obtained when the weight assignment algorithm is applied as reported in Section 4.2.4.3). If the pair of data sets are not significantly different, then we stop and set w_3 to be equal to w_t. Otherwise, we increment w_t by "1", and we repeat the experiment. Thus, the experiment is repeated until we find a weight at which the obtained cohesion values are not significantly different compared with those obtained when the weight is set to w_2 or when w_t reaches 2000. In the latter case, we assume that w_3 does not exist. Based on this experiment, w_3 is the first weight at which the obtained cohesion values are not significantly different from those obtained when the weight is set according to the proposed weight-assignment algorithm. The existing values of w_3 and the corresponding descriptive statistics of the obtained cohesion values are reported in Tables 4.8 – 4.12.

Table 4.11: Descriptive statistics for the considered measures applied to FreeMind.

Measure	Weight	Min	Max	25%	Med	75%	Mean	Std. Dev.
$LCOM_H$	w_1	0	2	0.50	0.92	1.13	0.84	0.57
	w_2	0	2	0.39	0.88	1.12	0.82	0.57
	$w_3 = 10$	0	2	0.42	0.90	1.10	0.83	0.57
Coh	w_1	0	1	0.17	0.62	1.00	0.60	0.39
	w_2	0	1	0.21	0.67	1.00	0.61	0.39
	$w_3 = 11$	0	1	0.20	0.67	1.00	0.61	0.39
LSCC	w_1	0	1	0.03	0.40	1.00	0.51	0.45
	w_2	0	1	0.04	0.48	1.00	0.52	0.45
	$w_3 = 1203$	0	1	0.03	0.48	1.00	0.52	0.45
CC	w_1	0	1	0.08	0.52	1.00	0.55	0.43
	w_2	0	1	0.08	0.54	1.00	0.56	0.43
	$w_3 = 1$	0	1	0.08	0.52	1.00	0.55	0.43
SCOM	w_1	0	1	0.06	0.50	1.00	0.55	0.44
	w_2	0	1	0.08	0.58	1.00	0.56	0.43
CAMC	w_1	0	1	0.00	0.25	0.39	0.24	0.24
	w_2	0	1	0.00	0.14	0.31	0.19	0.21
	$w_3 = 3$	0	1	0.00	0.18	0.29	0.19	0.21
NHD	w_1	0	1	0.63	0.77	1.00	0.74	0.28
	w_2	0	1	0.61	0.78	1.00	0.75	0.28

The results reported in Tables 4.8 – 4.12 regarding w_3 lead to the following observations:

- The weight w_3 existed for CAMC when applied to the Eclipse classes and for CC and NHD when applied to the

DrJava classes; it existed for all of the measures except for CC when applied to the Art of Illusion classes, all of the measures except for SCOM and NHD when applied to the FreeMind classes, and all of the measures except for CAMC when applied to the JHotDraw classes. In other words, w_3 exists for the majority of considered cases (i.e., 20 cases out of the considered 35 cases).

Table 4.12: Descriptive statistics for the considered measures applied to JHotDraw.

Measure	Weight	Min	Max	25%	Med	75%	Mean	Std. Dev.
$LCOM_H$	w_1	0	2	0.61	0.86	1.08	0.85	0.47
	w_2	0	2	0.57	0.83	1.07	0.83	0.47
	$w_3 = 4$	0	2	0.60	0.84	1.08	0.84	0.47
Coh	w_1	0	1	0.20	0.42	1.00	0.52	0.36
	w_2	0	1	0.22	0.46	1.00	0.53	0.36
	$w_3 = 4$	0	1	0.22	0.43	1.00	0.52	0.36
LSCC	w_1	0	1	0.04	0.17	1.00	0.40	0.41
	w_2	0	1	0.04	0.19	1.00	0.41	0.41
	$w_3 = 3$	0	1	0.04	0.17	1.00	0.40	0.41
CC	w_1	0	1	0.08	0.29	1.00	0.44	0.40
	w_2	0	1	0.08	0.30	1.00	0.45	0.40
	$w_3 = 3$	0	1	0.08	0.29	1.00	0.44	0.40
SCOM	w_1	0	1	0.09	0.32	1.00	0.46	0.40
	w_2	0	1	0.10	0.33	1.00	0.47	0.40
	$w_3 = 5$	0	1	0.10	0.32	1.00	0.46	0.40
CAMC	w_1	0	1	0.00	0.29	0.44	0.28	0.22
	w_2	0	1	0.00	0.22	0.36	0.23	0.20
NHD	w_1	0	1	0.60	0.76	0.92	0.73	0.24
	w_2	0	1	0.60	0.76	0.94	0.73	0.24
	$w_3 = 1$	0	1	0.60	0.76	0.92	0.73	0.24

- There was no measure for which the weight w_3 existed for all of the classes in all of the systems. For example, w_3 did not exist for the Eclipse and DrJava classes, and it existed for the classes of the other systems. Conversely, there is no measure for which the weight w_3 did not exist for all of the classes of all of the systems.

- Among the measures for which w_3 existed, the weight w_3 differs from the classes of one system to another, and it ranges widely, from 1 to 1203. Therefore, we rejected Null Hypothesis 2 and concluded that, given a specific cohesion measure, a constant weight considered in cohesion measurement will not yield cohesion values significantly similar to those obtained using the weight assignment algorithm.

4.2.4.5. Discussion

This empirical study involved four studies. The results of the first study demonstrated that a high percentage of attributes and parameters in the considered classes are of object types. This high percentage indicates the importance of considering the problem of whether to consider the encapsulated data in cohesion measurement. The attributes and parameters of object types potentially encapsulate other attributes that are ignored by existing cohesion measures. Thus, the high percentage of attributes/parameters of object types indicate that the values obtained using existing cohesion measures potentially do not represent the actual cohesion level, and they potentially mislead the decisions regarding practical applications such as predicting class fault-proneness, reusability, and maintainability.

As discussed in Section 4.2.1, the encapsulated data must be considered in cohesion measurement because these data are implicitly accessed or shared when the object is accessed or shared. However, accounting for DE increases the cohesion computation's complexity. Thus, if the consideration of DE causes the cohesion values to slightly change or to not change at all, then it would be worthless to consider DE in cohesion measurement. The second and third studies address this problem. The second study investigated the amount and direction of change in the cohesion values when the encapsulated data are considered, and the third study explored the significance of this change in the cohesion values.

The second study showed that the direction and amount of change due to the consideration of DE differs from one cohesion measure to another. The difference depends on the applied formula, the followed measuring approach, and the considered data. For example, the results showed that the measures that account for the access or share of attributes (i.e., $LCOM_H$, Coh, LSCC, CC, and SCOM) indicate a higher cohesion as the weight assigned to the attributes of object types increases. However, the measures that account for the types of parameters (i.e., CAMC and NHD) are affected differently. The mean CAMC value decreased as the weight of the parameter types increased. This relationship occurs because the average number of parameter types that appeared in the signatures of the methods in the considered classes is relatively low (i.e., its average among the considered systems ranges from 18% to 28%, as can be observed from the descriptive statistics given in Tables 4.8 – 4.12). In addition, as depicted in Figure 4.2, the percentage of parameters of object types is relatively high. These two factors caused the rate of increase in the numerator in CAMC's formula to be less than that for the denominator. The direction of change in NHD mean values differed from one system to another because the behavior of NHD is not necessarily monotonic with respect to the number of methods that have a parameter of a given type *j*.

The amount of change in mean values is affected by the cohesion measurement approach followed by the measure. That is, the mean values obtained by the measures based on counting the number of distinct attributes accessed by the methods (i.e., $LCOM_H$ and Coh) are affected more than those that are based on quantifying the degree of similarity between pairs of methods (i.e., LSCC, CC, and SCOM). This difference occurs because similarity-based measures are affected only when the attributes accessed by the methods are shared between the methods, whereas the values obtained using $LCOM_H$ and Coh are affected when the attributes are accessed by the methods even when such attributes are not shared between the methods. CAMC had the greatest change in the mean cohesion values when the weights were considered, due to its low values compared to other measures, which caused the rate of change in the CAMC denominator compared to that of its numerator to be much larger than the corresponding rates for the other measures. The amount of change in the mean values of NHD is relatively small because the NHD value of different classes can have opposite directions of change when the weights are considered. Thus, the effects for different classes eliminate each other when computing the average change in the NHD value.

The results of the third study showed that, with few exceptions, the consideration of the encapsulated data of the attributes and parameters in cohesion measurement caused the values obtained using the considered cohesion measures to significantly change. As discussed in Section 4.2.1, the consideration of DE in cohesion measurement is intuitively more appropriate than ignoring DE. Based on this fact and on the empirical result that the cohesion values obtained with and without the consideration of DE are significantly different, we conclude that it is more reliable to use the extended formulas to indicate the class cohesion. Using the original formulas potentially misleads software engineers when using the obtained values to indicate the class quality.

Assigning a constant weight to all of the attributes and parameters of object types is easier than applying the proposed weight assignment algorithm. However, the results of the fourth study show that there is no constant weight that consistently provides cohesion results that are not significantly different that those obtained when using the proposed weight-assignment algorithm. Therefore, the proposed algorithm must be used to provide cohesion values that properly consider the data encapsulated within the attributes and parameter types.

4.2.5. Summary

Class cohesion measures are intended to quantify the relationship between the attributes and methods in a class. Intuitively, in a certain class, a pair of methods that share an attribute of an object type is potentially more cohesive than those that share an attribute of a primitive type because the attribute of a reference type could implicitly refer to multiple data. Existing class cohesion measures ignore the implicit access to or sharing of attributes due to the encapsulation feature. As a result, the obtained cohesion values can be inaccurate and could lead to incorrect quality indications. Therefore, we demonstrated how to account for data encapsulation (DE) in cohesion measurement. To differentiate between attributes and parameters of different types, we listed a weight assignment algorithm. The weight that is assigned to an attribute or a parameter of a type depends on the number of directly or transitively encapsulated attributes of the type. Seven cohesion measures are extended to consider the assigned weights in cohesion measurement. These measures are the ones that are based on counting the number of accessed or shared attributes or parameter types.

The applicability and usefulness of the listed algorithm and measures are demonstrated by an empirical study, which involved five large-scale systems and seven cohesion measures. The empirical study investigated the impact of considering DE on the obtained cohesion values, and it led to several conclusions, as follows. The first conclusion is that it is important to study the impact of considering DE in cohesion measurement because a high percentage of attributes and parameters are of object types, and the consideration of their encapsulated data causes the cohesion values to significantly change for most of the considered classes and measures. This result indicates that the values that are obtained using existing cohesion measures are potentially unreliable, in some cases, and that they may not indicate cohesion properly because they ignore the implicit access or share of the encapsulated data that contributes to class cohesion. The results of the empirical study also show that it is risky to assign a constant value as a weight to all of the attributes and parameters of object types because of the absence of a constant weight that consistently leads to cohesion values that are not significantly different than the values obtained when assigning the weight according to the listed algorithm.

4.3. Accounting for Special Methods in Cohesion Measurement

4.3.1. Motivation

In object-oriented programming, some methods are typically provided to support the encapsulation key feature of the object-oriented paradigm. Some of these methods do not provide any functionality that contributes to the problem for which the class was developed. Instead, they are used to initialize attributes or inquire about their values. We refer to these methods as special methods, and we classify them into four different types, including constructors, destructors, access methods, and delegation methods. Constructors are used to initialize most or all of the attributes in the class and destructors are used to deinitialize most or all of the attributes. The access methods are classified as either setters or getters. A setter method initializes a single attribute and a getter method returns the reference/value of a single attribute. Finally, a delegation method is used to inquire about the status of a single attribute.

Each of these special methods has its own characteristics, which can artificially affect the class cohesion value. An incorrect determination of whether to include or exclude the special methods in the cohesion measurement can lead to improper re-designing decisions and actions that are based on the misleading class cohesion values that are obtained. However, the original definitions for most of the existing class cohesion measures do not differentiate between the different types of methods; therefore, these measures are ill-defined.

In this section, we qualitatively analyze the definitions and formulas of nineteen cohesion measures to investigate the impact of including/excluding each type of special methods on the values that can be obtained by the measures. The analysis is based on identifying typical cases that are featured by the special methods and analyzing the changes in the measured cohesion values for these cases. Such a theoretical qualitative analysis for the formulas of the measures helps in interpreting any related empirical results. In addition, the qualitative analysis provides a more general view for the possible scenarios in which the cohesion values are affected when the special methods are either included or excluded.

4.3.2. Cohesive Relations of Special Methods

The cohesion of a class is determined by the extent to which the attributes and methods of the class are directly or indirectly related. Typically, the existence of constructors and destructors in a class increases the number of direct and indirect relations in a class. Such an outcome occurs for two reasons: First, the constructors and destructors reference most, if not all, of the class attributes, which introduces additional direct relations to the class between each of the constructors and destructors and the class' attributes. Second, the attributes that are referenced by the constructors and destructors are typically referenced by some other methods in the class. Therefore, the existence of the constructors and destructors in the class creates indirect relations between them and the methods that reference the attributes. For the rest of this section, the discussion regarding the impact of including the constructors is applicable to the destructors as well because both types of methods are expected to reference the majority or all of the attributes.

The existence of access and delegation methods in a class increases the number of direct and indirect relations in a class due to the same two reasons that are mentioned above. However, since each access and delegation method typically references a single attribute, more relations are introduced by the constructors and destructors than by the access and delegation methods. Increasing the number of relations in a class by incorporating more attributes or methods does not necessarily increase a class's cohesion level. When assessing the cohesion level, both the existing relations and the missed possible relations must somehow be considered. For example, an access method has relations with the methods that reference the same accessed attribute, and it has no relations with the other methods. An access method references a single attribute; therefore, the number of methods that are related to the access method is typically less than the number of unrelated methods. As a result, the process of incorporating the access methods into the cohesion measurement is expected to reduce the obtained cohesion value.

Peer access and delegation methods are the setter, getter, and delegation methods that reference the same attribute. Non-peer access and delegation methods reference different attributes. Because access and delegation methods have the same characteristics, in terms of the number of referenced attributes (i.e., each access or delegation method references a single attribute), the discussion regarding the access methods also applies to delegation methods throughout the remainder of this study.

The impact of including all types of special methods in cohesion measurement on the cohesion values that are obtained is determined by the strength of the impact of each type of special method. In addition, it depends on the number of constructors, destructors, and access and delegation methods that are under consideration. That is, if the inclusion of the constructors and destructors increases the cohesion value that is obtained using a specific measure by an amount that is greater than the decrease in the cohesion value which is caused by including the access and delegation methods, then the cohesion value increases and vice versa.

A non-special method can reference any number of distinct attributes; however, typically, it references a lower number of distinct attributes in comparison to constructors and destructors. A non-special method may not reference any attributes, although, theoretically, this is an unusual case.

The existing cohesion measures use different approaches to measure cohesion. For example, some of the measures count the number of existing and missed relations in a class, and some of them are based on averaging the number of relations in a class. Some of the measures account only for direct relations, whereas others consider both direct and indirect relations. Some of the measures measure cohesion, and others measure the lack of cohesion in a class. Therefore, the effect of including special methods in a cohesion measurement varies according to the cohesion measure itself and the type of special method that is being considered (e.g., a constructor or an access method).

4.3.3. Qualitative Analysis

Here, we qualitatively study the impact of including or excluding special methods on the values that are obtained by applying each of the nineteen measures that are under consideration. This study is based on analyzing the definitions and formulas that are proposed for the measures. For each of the considered measures, the cases in which the inclusion of constructors and access methods causes the measure value to increase or decrease are identified and analyzed as follows.

4.3.3.1. $LCOM_{CK1}$

Unless a method shares an attribute with each of the other methods, including a method in the $LCOM_{CK1}$ measurement causes the $LCOM_{CK1}$ value to increase. This increase occurs because such an inclusion causes the number of pairs of methods that do not share attributes to increase. Ideally, the constructor shares an attribute with each other method, and, therefore, in this case, including the constructor does not affect the $LCOM_{CK1}$ value. There are two cases in which including the constructor affects the value of $LCOM_{CK1}$: (1) when the constructor references most of the attributes but not all of them, and some of the methods simultaneously only reference attributes that are not referenced by the constructor, or (2) when some of the methods do not reference any attributes. In either of these two unusual cases, including the constructor causes the $LCOM_{CK1}$ value to increase because the constructor does not share attributes with the indicated methods.

Non-peer access methods do not share attributes, and an access method is not expected to share attributes with all other methods. Therefore, including the access methods causes the number of method pairs that do not share attributes and, consequently, the $LCOM_{CK1}$ value to artificially increase. As a result, the recommendation is to include constructors and exclude access methods from the $LCOM_{CK1}$ measurement.

4.3.3.2. $LCOM_{CK2}$

When including a method in the $LCOM_{CK2}$ measurement, the change in the $LCOM_{CK2}$ value depends on the difference between the number of methods that do not share attributes with the included method and the number of methods that share attributes with the included method. Expectedly, this difference has a considerable negative value for a constructor method and a considerable positive value for an access method. Therefore, the inclusion of constructors or access methods is expected to artificially decrease or increase the $LCOM_{CK2}$ value, respectively. For the unusual cases that were described in Section 4.3.3.1, the inclusion of a constructor can increase the $LCOM_{CK2}$ value. As a result, when applying $LCOM_{CK2}$, the recommendation is to exclude constructors and access methods from the cohesion measurement.

4.3.3.3. $LCOM_L$ and $LCOM_{HM}$

Typically, including the constructor makes the class representative graph connected, which causes the $LCOM_L$ value to decrease to one. This is based on the typical expectation that each method in the class is referencing at least an attribute. However, when the class-representative graph is already connected, the inclusion of the constructor does not change the $LCOM_L$ value. In addition, when a method in the class does not share an attribute with any other method and also does not share an attribute with the constructor because of the same reasons that were indicated in Section 4.3.3.1, the inclusion of the constructor does not change the isolation situation of that method, although it may change the isolation situations of other methods that do not feature the same unusual cases. As a result, the inclusion of constructors typically decreases the $LCOM_L$ value of the class.

The inclusion of an access method causes the $LCOM_L$ value to increase only when, unusually, the access method does not share attributes with any other method in the class. Otherwise, typically, the $LCOM_L$ value remains the same when including access methods. Note that the inclusion of an access method does not complicate the $LCOM_L$ computation because this measure is based on simply counting the number of disjointed components. $LCOM_L$ and $LCOM_{HM}$ share the same arguments because constructors and access methods do not typically invoke other methods. As a result, when applying either $LCOM_L$ or $LCOM_{HM}$, the recommendation is to include access methods and exclude constructors from the cohesion measurement.

4.3.3.4. $LCOM_H$

Including the constructor does not change the numerator part of the $LCOM_H$ formula, which is given in Chapter 2, when the constructor accesses all attributes. This is because the value of a (i.e., the summation of the number of distinct attributes that are referenced by each method in the class) in the formula is increased by l (i.e., the number of attributes in the class), and the value of k (i.e., the number of considered methods) is increased by one; hence, $(k+1)\times l-(a+l)=kl-a$. The inclusion of a constructor slightly increases the numerator when the constructor accesses most of the attributes. However, the inclusion of a constructor causes the denominator part to increase by l. Therefore, the inclusion of a constructor potentially causes the $LCOM_H$ value to artificially decrease.

The inclusion of an access method causes the numerator and denominator parts of the formula to increase by the values of (l-

1) and l, respectively. This means that the inclusion of access methods causes the $LCOM_H$ value to slightly increase or decrease depending on the values of k, l, and a. Note that including the access methods does not complicate the $LCOM_H$ computation because $LCOM_H$ is based on simply counting the number of distinct attributes that are referenced by each method. As a result, the recommendation is to include access methods and exclude constructors from the $LCOM_H$ measurement.

4.3.3.5. LSCC

LSCC can be calculated it two ways, either by using the direct formula given in Section II or by obtaining the ratio of the summation of the similarities between all pairs of methods to the total number of pairs of methods. The similarity between a pair of methods is determined by dividing the number of shared attributes between the two methods by the total number of attributes in the class. The similarity between a constructor and any other method m is expected to be higher than the similarity between method m and any other method in the class. As a result, the inclusion of a constructor method artificially increases the LSCC value.

The similarity between an access method and any other non-peer access method is zero, and it is low (i.e., has a value of $1/l$) between peer access methods. In addition, the similarity between an access method and any other method has a maximum value of $1/l$, whereas, generally, the maximum possible similarity between a pair of methods is one. Therefore, the inclusion of access methods is expected to artificially reduce the LSCC value. As a result, when applying LSCC, the recommendation is to exclude constructors and access methods from the cohesion measurement.

4.3.3.6. CC

The similarity definition of CC differs from that of LSCC in the sense that the similarity between a pair of methods is the ratio of the number of shared attributes between the two methods to the total number of distinct attributes that are referenced by either of the two methods. As a result, the similarity between a constructor method and another method depends on the percentage *p* of attributes that are accessed by the other method. That is, if the value of *p* is relatively high, then the similarity will be relatively high, and vice versa. Typically, *p* is not high for methods other than the constructor, and, therefore, the inclusion of a constructor is expected to decrease the value of CC from this perspective. However, from a different point of view, because the constructor references most or all of the attributes, the chance that the constructor is similar in some degree to other methods is higher than that for a pair of non-special methods. It is important to remember that methods that do share common attributes have a similarity of degree zero. Therefore, from this perspective, including a constructor can cause the CC value to increase. As a result, these two points of view oppositely impact the CC value, and they depend on factors that vary from one class to another. As a result, the impact of including the constructor in the CC computation does not follow a specific trend. Instead, it depends on the relations between the nonspecial methods.

For example, assume that a class *C* consists of three attributes: a constructor and two other methods. If each of the two methods references the same single attribute, then the similarity between the two methods will have a value of 1. If the constructor is excluded from the CC computation, then the CC value will equal the value of the similarity between the two methods (i.e., a value of 1). If the constructor references the three class attributes, then the similarity between the constructor and each of the two methods will have a value of 0.33, as defined by the CC measure. In this case, the value of the CC measure will be 0.55 (i.e., [0.33+0.33+1]/2); hence, the value of the CC decreases from the value of 1 to the value of 0.55. In another hypothetical example, assume that a class has the same number of attributes and methods as class *C*; the constructor references all the attributes, and each of the attributes references two attributes, such that one of the attributes is commonly referenced by the two methods. In this case, the similarity between the two methods is 0.33, and the similarity between the constructor and each method is 0.67. If the constructor is excluded from the CC computation, then the CC value will equal the value of the similarity between the two nonspecial methods (i.e., 0.33), whereas the CC value increases from 0.33 to 0.56 (i.e., [0.67+0.67+0.33]/2) when the constructor is considered in the CC computation.

The similarity between an access method and any (1) non-peer access method is zero, (2) peer access method is one (i.e., maximum), and (3) other method depends on the attributes that are accessed by that other method. If the other method shares the same attribute with the access method, then the similarity will be one in the event that the other method accesses only an attribute. In addition, it will linearly decrease as the number of attributes that are accessed by the other method increases. This means that the impact of including the access methods is not generally determined; the inclusion of access methods causes the CC value to increase in some typical cases and to decrease in some other typical cases. As a result, the recommendation is to exclude constructors and access methods from the CC measurement.

4.3.3.7. SCOM

The similarity definition for SCOM is more complicated than that for LSCC and CC. Here, the similarity between two methods depends on three factors. The similarity is proportional to (1) the number of shared attributes and (2) the relative number of distinct attributes that are accessed by either of the two methods, and it is reversely proportional to the minimum number of attributes that are accessed by each method. When measuring the similarity between a constructor and another method, the first and third factors will eliminate the effects of one another if the constructor references all of the attributes that are referenced by the method. As a result, the similarity between a constructor and another method depends on the second factor (i.e., the relative number of distinct attributes that are referenced by the constructor), which is typically high. Therefore, including the constructor potentially causes the SCOM value to artificially increase.

The similarity between an access method and a non-peer access method is zero, and it is equal to $1/l$ for a pair of peer access methods. The similarity between an access method and another method equals zero when the pair of methods does not share a common attribute. In addition, it is equal to the relative number of attributes that are accessed by the other method when the pair of methods share a common attribute. In other words, the similarity between an access method and another method is usually low, and it is only high in one unusual case when the other method references a high relative number of attributes that include the attribute that is referenced by the access method. As a result, the inclusion of the access method is expected to artificially decrease the SCOM value. In conclusion, the recommendation is to exclude both of the constructors and access methods from the SCOM measurement.

4.3.3.8. Coh

Typically, including the constructor artificially increases the average number of distinct attributes that are accessed by each method in the class, which consequently artificially increases the Coh value. In contrast, access methods artificially decrease the Coh value because they decrease the average number of distinct attributes that are accessed by each method in the class. As a result, when applying Coh, the recommendation is to exclude both constructors and access methods from the cohesion measurement.

4.3.3.9. TCC, LCC, DC_D, and DC_I

The constructor potentially references a number of attributes to a greater extent than any other non-special methods. Therefore, the chance for a constructor method to be directly or transitively connected to other methods is higher than that for non-special methods. As a result, the inclusion of the constructor artificially increases the TCC and LCC values. In this case, the LCC value is expected to increase at a rate that is higher than that for TCC. This is because the constructor is not only expected to be directly connected to each other method, but it also causes some other methods to be transitively connected to one another.

Pairs of access methods are not directly connected, except for peer access methods. In addition, the number of methods to which an access method is directly connected is potentially fewer than that for other non-special methods. Therefore, including access methods is expected to artificially decrease the TCC value.

In usual cases, the attributes are not supposed to be only referenced by access methods but also by other non-special methods. In this case, the access method is directly connected to the peer access method and the special methods that directly reference the same attribute. In addition, it can be transitively connected to other non-special methods and non-peer access methods in a manner that greatly depends on how the other methods are connected to one another. For example, assume that a class has an access method *m1*, two other methods *m2* and *m3*, and two attributes *a1* and *a2*. If *a1* is only referenced by *m1*, and if *a2* is referenced by both *m2* and *m3*, then including the access method in the LCC measurement decreases the LCC value from 1 to 0.33. In another hypothetical scenario, if *a1* is referenced by *m1* and *m2*, and if *a2* is only referenced by *m3*, then including the access method in the LCC computation increases the LCC value from zero to 0.33. As a result, the effect of including the access methods in the LCC value depends on how the other methods are related to each other and to the access methods. Therefore, the access method can considerably increase or decrease the value of the LCC.

The difference between DC_D and TCC as well as DC_I and LCC is in the consideration of the references of attributes that derive from method invocations. As previously indicated, constructors and access methods typically do not invoke other methods. Therefore, the above discussion regarding TCC and LCC similarly applies to DC_D and DC_I, respectively. As a result, when applying TCC, LCC, DC_D, or DC_I, the recommendation is to exclude both constructors and access methods from the cohesion measurement.

4.3.3.10. CBMC

The CBMC value is proportional to the minimum number of glue methods (i.e., the minimum number of methods for which removal causes the class-representative graph to become disjointed) and is inversely proportional to the number of considered methods. When the constructor is considered, it will be the best candidate method to be included in the minimum set of glue methods because, typically, the constructor references all attributes. In this case, if the graph, without including the constructor, is connected and then the constructor is included, the minimum set of glue methods will include the constructor and the glue methods of the original graph. Unless the original graph is fully connected, the minimum number of glue methods of the original graph will be fewer than the number of methods that are represented in the graph. Therefore, the CBMC value increases when a method is added, and that method increases the number of glue methods by one, which is the case when a constructor that references all attributes is added. It is important to note that when one or more of the methods do not reference attributes, and, thus, the class-representative graph is disjointed and the CBMC value of the class is zero, the inclusion of the constructor does not change the CBMC value even if the constructor references all of the attributes.

The inclusion of nodes that represent access methods to a connected class-representative graph does not change the minimum set of glue methods. This is because, in this case, the attribute that is referenced by the access method is also referenced by some other methods. Therefore, the removal of the access method does not make the connected graph disjointed. However, the inclusion of access methods increases the number of considered methods and, thus, decreases the CBMC value. As a result, the recommendation is to exclude both constructors and access methods from the CBMC cohesion measurement.

4.3.3.11. PCCC

PCCC is based on counting the number of simple paths from each node to each other node in the class-representative graph. The number of simple paths that are initiated from a node that represents a method greatly depends on the number of attributes that are referenced by that method. Therefore, the inclusion of the constructor increases the average number of simple paths and consequently increases the PCCC value because the constructor references most or all of the attributes in the class. Oppositely, the inclusion of access methods decreases the average number of simple paths and, consequently, decreases the PCCC value because each access method references a single attribute. As a result, the recommendation is to exclude both constructors and access methods from the PCCC measurement.

4.3.3.12. OL_n

The OL_n value depends on the average strength of the class attributes. The strength of an attribute depends on the total strengths of the methods that reference this attribute. Recursively, the strength of each method depends on the total strengths of the attributes that are referenced by the method. Consequently, the constructor potentially has the highest strength because it references all or most of the attributes, and, therefore, when the constructor is considered, the attributes that are connected to the constructor have an average strength that is higher than that when the constructor is excluded. In other words, including the constructor potentially increases the OL_n value.

An access method is connected to one attribute, and, therefore, it has a relatively low strength, which consequently lowers the strength of the accessed attribute. On average, when the access methods are considered, the attributes that are referenced by access methods are expected to have lower strengths than those when the access methods are excluded. Therefore, the inclusion of access methods potentially decreases the OL_n value. Similar to CBMC, the OL_n value for a class with a disjointed representative graph is zero. Therefore, OL_n has effects that are similar to those that are specified for CBMC when the nodes that represent the constructors or access methods are added to an already disjointed graph. As a result, the recommendation is to exclude both constructors and access methods from the OL_n measurement.

4.3.3.13. CAMC

CAMC is based on an assumption that the types of method parameters are potentially the same as the types of the attributes that are referenced by the methods. Based on this assumption, the inclusion of a constructor that has parameters that are used to initialize all of the attributes increases the average number of distinct types of parameters of all methods, which increases the CAMC value.

A setter method has one parameter type, whereas a getter method does not have any parameter type. Therefore, the inclusion of access methods potentially decreases the CAMC value. As a result, the recommendation is to exclude both constructors and access methods from the CAMC measurement.

4.3.3.14. NHD

NHD is based on averaging the agreement degree between each pair of methods, wherein the agreement degree of a pair of methods is inversely proportional to the number of parameter types that are used by only one of the methods. The assumption about the relationship between the parameter and attribute types is similar to that used in CAMC. The constructor is expected to have many more parameter types than any of the other methods. Therefore, the agreement between the constructor and other methods is expected to be low, which consequently reduces the NHD value.

Similarly, the matching between the parameter types of the access methods and other methods is expected to be low. However, the agreement does not only consider the types of the parameters of the two considered methods, but it also considers all of the types of parameters of all methods. Access methods and other methods agree in that they do not have other parameter types aside from their own parameters. In addition, if the number of such parameters is relatively high, as expected, the agreement between the access methods and other methods is expected to be relatively high, which increases the NHD value. As a result, the recommendation is to exclude both constructors and access methods from the NHD measurement.

4.3.3.15. MMAC

This measure has the same assumption as that for CAMC and is based on measuring the similarities between methods in terms of parameter type matches if these types also match the attribute types. The average similarity between a constructor and each other method is expected to be higher than that between each pair of other methods. Therefore, including constructors potentially increases the MMAC value.

Opposite to LSCC, which is based on the same similarity concept, setter methods that have the same parameter types have some degree of similarity, although they reference different attributes. MMAC does not only consider the types of the parameters but also considers the return type of the method. Therefore, getter methods that have the same return type feature some degree of similarity among themselves and between themselves and other setter methods that have the same parameter types, including peer access methods. Finally, access methods for which the parameter types match the parameter types of other methods have some degree of similarity, although they may reference different attributes as long as the attributes have the same types. All of these factors potentially cause the

MMAC value to increase if the average similarity that is caused by these factors when the access method is included is higher than the average similarity that is featured in the class before including the access methods. Otherwise, the MMAC value increases or remains the same. As a result, the impact of including the access methods on the MMAC value cannot be generally determined, and such an inclusion considerably changes the value of MMAC in some typical cases. In conclusion, the recommendation is to exclude both constructors and access methods from the MMAC measurement.

4.3.4. Empirical Analysis for the Cohesion Values

We empirically studied the impact of including special methods on the values that were obtained using the nineteen cohesion measures discussed in Section 4.3.3. The goal of this study was to empirically determine whether the changes in the cohesion values are significant, and consequently, to empirically determine whether it is important for software practitioners to pay attention to the problem of including/excluding special methods when using cohesion measures in supporting software quality decisions. Four scenarios were considered: (1) excluding all special methods, (2) including constructors and excluding access methods, (3) including access methods and excluding constructors, and (4) excluding all special methods.

Five Java open-source software systems from different domains were selected, including Art of Illusion v.2.5 (Illusion 2025), FreeMind v.0.8.0 (FreeMind 2025), GanttProject v.2.0.5 (GanttProject 2025), JabRef v.2.3 beta 2 (JabRef 2025), and Openbravo v.0.0.24 (Openbravo 2025). Art of Illusion consists of 463 classes and is a 3-D modeling, rendering, and animation studio system. FreeMind consists of 379 classes and is a hierarchical editing system. GanttProject consists of 435 classes and is a project-scheduling application that features resource management, calendaring, and importing and exporting (MS Project, HTML, PDF, spreadsheets). JabRef consists of 540 classes and is a graphical application for managing bibliographical databases. Openbravo consists of 428 classes and is a point-of-sale application that is designed for touch screens. We selected these five open-source systems from http://sourceforge.net. The restrictions that were placed on the choice of these systems were that they (1) be implemented using Java, (2) be relatively large in terms of the number of classes, (3) be from different domains, and (4) have available source code and fault repositories.

We developed our own Java tool to automate the cohesion measurement process for Java classes using the nineteen cohesion measures that are considered in this section. The tool (1) analyzed the Java source code, (2) extracted the source code information that is required by the nineteen measures to calculate cohesion values, (3) identified the constructors and access methods, and (4) calculated cohesion values for each of the four versions of each class. Each version features one of the scenarios that were indicated earlier in this section. The tool was applied to each class in the five systems, which implied applying the tool on the 2,245 considered classes. The tool only measures cohesion of Java classes, and therefore, the empirical studies reported in this study do not investigate the impact of including destructors, as they are not supported by Java. In addition, it is difficult to automate the detection of delegation methods because delegation methods are highly dependent on the semantics of the problem.

The empirical studies consider both constructors and access methods because these two types of methods can be detected automatically. The tool considers a method to be a constructor if the method does not have a declared return type and the name of the method matches the name of the class. An access method can be a getter or a setter. The tool considers a method to be a setter for a variable *var* if the method has a name set*Var*, has a void return type, and assigns the value passed as a parameter to the variable *var*. A method is considered as a getter for a variable *var* if the method has the name get*Var*, has a return type that matches the type of the variable *var*, and returns the value of *var*. Because destructors and delegation methods were not considered in the empirical studies, the rest of this section will use the term "special methods" to refer only to the considered types of special methods (i.e., constructors and access methods).

For each of the four considered scenarios, Table 4.13 lists the descriptive statistics for the number of methods in the classes considered, including the minimum, the 25% quartile, the mean, the median, the 75% quartile, the maximum value, and the standard deviation. In addition, Figures 4.4, 4.5, and 4.6 depict the relative frequencies of the number of constructors, access methods, and special methods considered, respectively, that were included in the classes considered.

Table 4.13: Descriptive statistics for the methods of the classes considered.

Scenario	Min	Max	25%	Med	75%	Mean	Std. Dev.
Excluding all considered special methods	0	125	1	3	7	4.93	6.51
Including constructors	0	126	2	4	8	5.90	6.68
Including access and delegation methods	0	125	1	4	8	6.20	7.95
Including all considered special methods	1	126	2	5	9	7.17	8.15

Figure 4.4 demonstrates that some of the classes (24.1%) do not have constructors, most of the classes (63.2%) have a single constructor, and each of the rest of the classes (12.7%) has multiple constructors. When considering constructors, Table 4.13 demonstrates that the average number of methods in a class increases by 19.7%, from 4.93 to 5.90.

Figure 4.5 demonstrates that more than half of the classes do not include access methods. When considering access methods, Table 4.13 demonstrates that the average number of methods in a class increases by 25.8%, from 4.93 to 6.2. Finally, Figure 4.7

demonstrates that most of the considered classes (80.4%) include special methods, and Table 4.13 shows that when considering all special methods, the average number of methods in a class increases considerably, by 45.4%, from 4.93 to 7.17. This high percentage for special methods indicates the importance of studying their impact on the cohesion values that are obtained by the measures. In addition, the high percentage of special methods potentially indicates that a measure will incorrectly indicate the degree of cohesion when all of the methods are considered if that measure is supposed to only consider nonspecial methods.

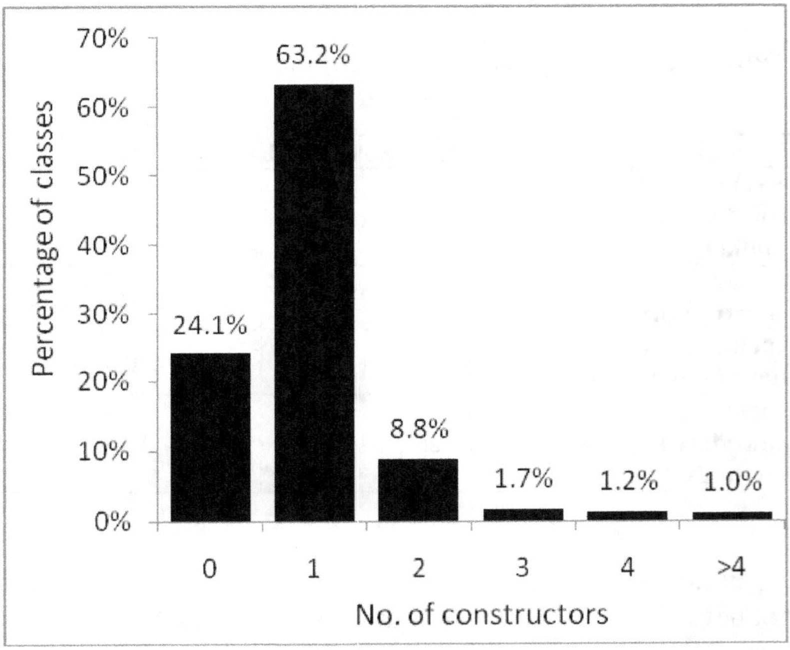

Figure 4.4: The distribution of constructors.

Some of the measures considered are undefined for some classes. For example, TCC, LCC, DC_D, DC_I, CC, SCOM, $LCOM_H$, and NHD are undefined for classes that consist of fewer than two methods. In addition, $LCOM_H$, SCOM, Coh, and NHD are undefined for classes without any attributes. The cohesion measure applicability problem has been thoroughly discussed in Section 4.1. Our empirical studies do not attempt to compare the results across the nineteen measures. Instead, the studies seek to compare the results across the four scenarios for each measure alone. Therefore, when considering each measure, we obtained the cohesion results for all of the considered classes in all of the four scenarios, excluding the classes for which at least one of the scenarios resulted in an undefined cohesion value when the considered measure was applied. We then compared the respective results of the remaining classes. The classes for which at least one of the scenarios resulted in an undefined cohesion value were excluded so that we could perform the same analysis on the same set of classes and, therefore, could compare the respective results in an unbiased manner.

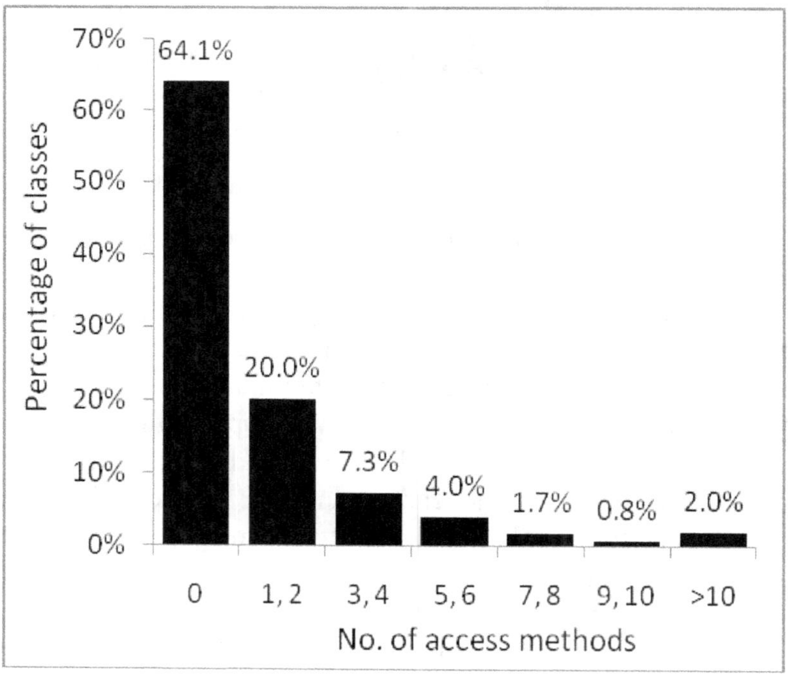

Figure 4.5: The distribution of access methods.

For each of the four scenarios considered, we obtained mean values. Tables 4.14 and 4.15 depict the number of classes for which each measure is defined and the means of the cohesion values of the measures considered when they were applied in the four aforementioned scenarios.

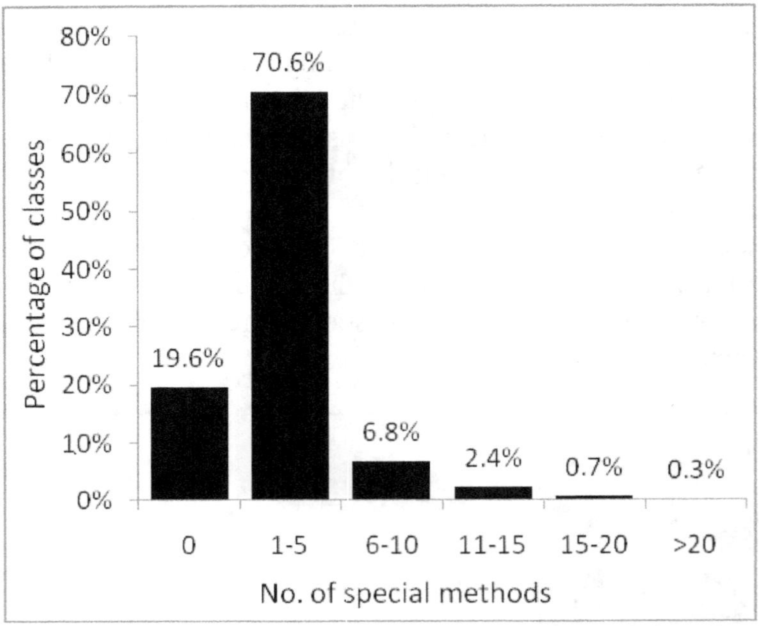

Figure 4.6: The distribution of the considered special methods.

To investigate whether the changes in the cohesion values were statistically significant, we applied the paired z-test (Hines et al. 2003), a standard statistical technique applied to compare two independent sets of samples. We applied this technique because the cohesion values before and after considering the special methods are independent and the number of selected classes is large enough. In our context, to apply the paired z-test for a measure, (1) the difference between the cohesion values before and after the change has to be calculated for each class, (2) the means and standard deviation values of these differences have to be obtained, and (3) the Z value has to be calculated by multiplying the mean of the differences by the square root of the number of classes and dividing the result by the standard deviation of the differences. We applied the typical significance threshold ($\alpha = 0.05$) to decide whether the differences between the cohesion values were significant. The corresponding critical Z value is 1.96. The differences were considered significant when the absolute value of Z was greater than that of the critical Z. We applied this analysis to compare the values of Scenarios 2, 3, and 4 to the values of Scenario 1. The analysis results, including the mean of the differences and the Z values, are listed in Tables 4.14 and 4.15. These results lead to the following observations:

Table 4.14: Paired z-test results and partial descriptive statistics for the measures considered (for Scenarios 1 and 2).

Metric	No. of considered classes	Scenario 1: Excluding special methods	Scenario 2: Including constructors		
		Mean	Mean	Mean Diff.	Z
$LCOM_{CK1}$	1651	34.20	38.61	-4.41	-14.21
$LCOM_{CK2}$	1651	27.31	29.56	-2.25	-8.48
$LCOM_{L}$	2245	1.65	1.55	0.10	7.53
$LCOM_{HM}$	2245	1.64	1.54	0.10	7.13
$LCOM_{H}$	1281	0.88	0.77	0.11	18.44
LSCC	2245	0.32	0.32	0.01	**0.85**
CC	1281	0.20	0.22	-0.02	-4.43
SCOM	1281	0.23	0.26	-0.03	-7.43
Coh	1579	0.39	0.43	-0.03	-11.11
CBMC	1579	0.18	0.17	0.01	**1.24**
OL_2	1579	0.17	0.17	<0.01	**0.85**
PCCC	2245	0.39	0.28	0.11	17.17
TCC	1651	0.34	0.36	-0.01	-4.01
LCC	1651	0.38	0.41	-0.03	-6.47
DC_D	1651	0.35	0.36	-0.01	-3.89
DC_I	1651	0.38	0.41	-0.03	-6.37
CAMC	2245	0.71	0.59	0.12	39.28
NHD	1372	0.52	0.58	-0.06	-15.77
MMAC	2245	0.16	0.10	0.06	6.58

- The cohesion values for most of the measures considered changed significantly when any type of special method was included in the cohesion measurement. The few insignificantly changed values are highlighted in boldface in Tables 4.14 and 4.15.

Table 4.15: Paired z-test results and partial descriptive statistics for the measures considered (for Scenarios 3 and 4).

Metric	No. of consid-ered classes	Scenario 3: Including access methods			Scenario 4: Including special methods		
		Mean	Mean Diff.	Z	Mean	Mean Diff.	Z
$LCOM_{CK1}$	1651	51.79	-17.59	-8.02	57.27	-23.1	-9.5
$LCOM_{CK2}$	1651	40.42	-13.11	-6.70	42.73	-15.4	-7.4
$LCOM_L$	2245	1.79	-0.14	-6.50	1.62	<0.01	**1.7**
$LCOM_{HM}$	2245	1.77	-0.13	-6.13	1.62	<0.01	**1.3**
$LCOM_H$	1281	0.83	0.05	9.85	0.75	0.1	18.1
LSCC	2245	0.31	0.02	3.19	0.30	<0.01	4.8
CC	1281	0.20	<0.01	**0.58**	0.21	<0.01	-2.9
SCOM	1281	0.23	<0.01	**1.85**	0.26	<0.01	-6.0
Coh	1579	0.39	<0.01	**0.43**	0.42	<0.01	-6.7
CBMC	1579	0.16	0.02	7.41	0.16	<0.01	4.5
OL_2	1579	0.16	0.02	7.19	0.15	<0.01	4.6
PCCC	2245	0.34	0.05	11.62	0.25	0.1	19.6
TCC	1651	0.33	0.01	3.36	0.35	<0.01	**-1.7**
LCC	1651	0.40	-0.02	-6.58	0.43	-0.1	-11.8
DC_D	1651	0.34	0.01	3.45	0.35	<0.01	**-1.5**
DC_I	1651	0.40	-0.02	-6.50	0.44	-0.1	-11.6
CAMC	2245	0.67	0.04	18.95	0.55	0.2	45.1
NHD	1372	0.57	-0.05	-14.62	0.62	-0.1	-21.2
MMAC	2245	0.15	0.01	**1.73**	0.09	0.1	8.7

- The value and sign of the mean of the differences vary from one measure to another depending on the definition of the measure, as discussed in Section 4.3.3. However, the qualitative and empirical analysis results do not always identically match. For example, qualitatively, when constructors are included in $LCOM_{CK1}$ measurement, the cohesion values will not be changed. This relationship is based on the ideal case in which each constructor references all of the attributes in the class of interest, which is not always true in practice. For the selected classes, we found that the constructors, the access methods, and the nonspecial methods reference an average of 61.7%, 37.1%, and 39.3% of the attributes, respectively.

- The results for a few measures demonstrate that the cohesion values were not significantly changed when some types of special methods were added. The z-test analysis considers the signs of the changes in the cohesion values. For example, if the value changes positively for a class and negatively by the same amount for another class, the mean difference will be zero, and the value will be considered to be changed insignificantly. Therefore, in a z-test analysis, the values are considered to be insignificantly changed if the magnitudes of the changes are small or if the changes have different signs such that the changes are eliminating each other when considering all of the samples together. Therefore, to explore the reason why a few of the measures show insignificant change when including special methods, we calculated the percentage of the average absolute change in the cohesion values for all of the classes. For example, to obtain the percentage of the average absolute change for LSCC in Scenario 2, we (1) calculated, for each class considered, the absolute difference between the LSCC values in Scenarios 1 and 2, (2) obtained the average of these differences over all classes, and (3) found the percentage of this average to the mean value for Scenario 1 (0.32). To obtain the percentage of average absolute changes for Scenario 3, we considered the absolute differences between the values obtained in Scenarios 1 and 3. Similarly, to obtain the percentage of average absolute changes for Scenario 4, we considered the absolute differences between the values obtained in Scenarios 1 and 4. The results show that for the few changed values whose changes are insignificant, the average absolute change ranges from 11.4% to 44.4%. These changes are greater than the corresponding values for some other measures that have significant changes. This observation demonstrates that the insignificant changes in the values shown for some of the measures in Tables 4.14 and 4.15 are because of the sign difference of the change in the cohesion values across the classes considered.

- The results of the fourth scenario are affected by the strength and significance of the impact of each type of special method. If the obtained values of a specific measure in both the second and third scenarios significantly change with the same trend (i.e., if the mean values in both scenarios either increase or decrease), then the obtained cohesion values in the fourth scenario will significantly change with the same trend of both the second and third scenarios. For example, the results show that including each of constructors and access methods causes the $LCOM_{CK1}$ values to increase significantly. Therefore, in the fourth scenario, when both types of special methods are considered together, the $LCOM_{CK1}$ values follow the same trend of increasing significantly. The same observation applies for $LCOM_{CK2}$, $LCOM_{H}$, PCCC, LCC, DC_{I}, CAMC, and NHD. When the cohesion values for both the second and third scenarios follow the same trend of change, but one of them is changed significantly and the other changes only slightly, then the values in the fourth scenario will change significantly, along with the same trend as the other two scenarios. This observation applies for LSCC, CBMC, OL_{2}, and MMAC. On the other hand, if the second and third scenarios have opposite effects on the cohesion values (i.e., if one of them causes the cohesion values to increase and the other one causes the values to decrease), then in the fourth scenario, the two opposite effects will partially eliminate each other. Therefore, if the two opposite effects have close strengths, then the change of the cohesion values in the fourth scenario can be insignificant (e.g., as for the $LCOM_{L}$, $LCOM_{HM}$, TCC, and DC_{D} measures). Otherwise, the change in the cohesion values will follow the trend of the scenario that has the stronger effect (e.g., as for CC, SCOM, and Coh measures).

In summary, the empirical results reported in this section demonstrate the importance of addressing the problem of including or excluding special methods because these results show that a high percentage of classes include special methods.

In addition, the results indicate that including special methods in cohesion measurement significantly changes the cohesion values for most of the measures considered, which might affect the use of the cohesion measures in practice.

Based on the obtained results and the discussion provided in Section 4.3.2, if the inclusion of constructors in the cohesion measurement significantly affects the results of an application to which the cohesion was empirically determined to be related, then the constructors should be included in the cohesion measurement. Otherwise, the application will be missing a factor that is related to the cohesion aspects. On the other hand, if the inclusion of access methods in the cohesion measurement significantly affects the results of an application to which the cohesion was empirically determined to be related, then the access methods should be excluded from the cohesion measurement. Otherwise, the application will be incorrectly influenced by factors that are unrelated to the cohesion aspects.

4.3.5. Summary

This section qualitatively explored the impact of including or excluding special methods in cohesion measurement with respect to the cohesion values that are obtained. The exploration is based on analyzing the impact of including the special methods on the definitions and formulas that are applied via nineteen cohesion measures. Table 4.15 summarizes the expected changes in the cohesion values when the special methods are included in cohesion measurement. The qualitative analysis that is reported in this section leads to several observations as follows. When using most of the considered measures, the cohesion (lack of cohesion) value of a class increases (decreases) when the constructors and destructors are considered in the cohesion measurement. When using most of the considered measures, the cohesion (lack of cohesion) value of a class decreases (increases) when the access and delegation methods are considered in the cohesion measurement. These two observations are consistent with the intuition that was discussed in Section 4.3.2.

Table 4.15: Expected changes in cohesion values based on theoretical grounds.

Measure	Impact of including constructors and destructors on measure values	Impact of including access and delegation methods on measure values
$LCOM_{CK1}$	Increases for unusual cases but, otherwise, remains the same	Increases
LSCC, SCOM, Coh, TCC, DC_D, CBMC, PCCC, OL_n, and CAMC	Increases	Decreases
$LCOM_{CK2}$ and NHD	Decreases	Increases
$LCOM_L$ and $LCOM_{HM}$	Decreases	Increases for unusual cases but, otherwise, remains the same
$LCOM_H$	Decreases	Slightly increases or decreases
LCC, DC_I, and MMAC	Increases	Depends on other factors
CC	Depends on other factors	Decreases

The recommendation to include or exclude the special methods in the cohesion measurement greatly depends on the application of interest for which the cohesion value will be used. For example, when using the cohesion values to predict whether the class requires refactoring, the constructors and destructors must be included. This is because the constructors and destructors are used to partially provide the class' intended functionality. On the other hand, the access and delegation methods must be excluded because they are used not to provide functionalities, but instead, to support encapsulation. Therefore, the access and delegation methods are not expected to weaken the class design and cause the class to be refactored. Changing the cohesion value of a class because of the inclusion or exclusion of access or delegation methods can alter the value and mislead the refactoring decision.

Portions of this chapter are adapted from the following papers *(reproduced with permission from the publishers)*:

- J. Al Dallal, Improving the applicability of object-oriented class cohesion metrics, Information and Software Technology, 2011, Vol. 53, No. 9, pp. 914-928.
- J. Al Dallal, The impact of accounting for special methods in the measurement of object-oriented class cohesion on refactoring and fault prediction activities, Journal of Systems and Software, 2012, Vol. 85, No. 5, pp. 1042-1057.
- J. Al Dallal, Qualitative analysis for the impact of accounting for special methods in object-oriented class cohesion measurement, Journal of Software, 2013, Vol. 8. No. 2, pp. 327-336. © Academy Publisher
- J. Al Dallal, Accounting for data encapsulation in the measurement of object-oriented class cohesion, Journal of Software: Evolution and Process, Vol. 27, No. 5, 2015, pp. 373-400.

BIBLIOGRAPHY

J. Al Dallal, Mathematical validation of object-oriented class cohesion metrics, International Journal of Computers, 2010, Vol. 4, No. 2, pp. 45-52.

J. Al Dallal, Improving the applicability of object-oriented class cohesion metrics, Information and Software Technology, 2011, Vol. 53, No. 9, pp. 914-928.

J. Al Dallal, Measuring the discriminative power of object-oriented class cohesion metrics, IEEE Transactions on Software Engineering, 2011, Vol. 37, No. 6, pp. 788-804.

J. Al Dallal, Transitive-based object-oriented lack-of-cohesion metric, Procedia Computer Science, 2011, Vol. 3, pp. 1581-1587.

J. Al Dallal, Assessing the discriminative power of object-oriented cohesion metrics in practice, 2nd World Conference on Information Technology, Antalya, Turkey, 2011.

J. Al Dallal, Theoretical analysis for the impact of including special methods in lack-of-cohesion computation, 1st World Conference on Innovation and Software Development, Istanbul, Turkey, 2011.

J. Al Dallal, Improving object-oriented lack-of-cohesion metric by excluding special methods, proceedings of the 10th WSEAS International Conference on Software Engineering, Parallel and Distributed Systems (SEPADS 2011), Cambridge, UK, February 2011.

J. Al Dallal, Fault prediction and the discriminative powers of connectivity-based object-oriented class cohesion metrics, Information and Software Technology, 2012a, Vol. 54, No. 4, pp. 396-416.

J. Al Dallal, The impact of accounting for special methods in the measurement of object-oriented class cohesion on refactoring and fault prediction activities, Journal of Systems and Software, 2012b, Vol. 85, No. 5, pp. 1042-1057.

J. Al Dallal, Constructing models for predicting extract subclass refactoring opportunities using object-oriented quality metrics, Information and Software Technology, 2012b, Vol. 54, No. 10, pp. 1125-1141.

J. Al Dallal, The impact of inheritance on the internal quality attributes of java classes, Kuwait Journal of Science and Engineering, 2012, Vol. 39, No. 2A, pp. 131-154.

J. Al Dallal, Qualitative analysis for the impact of accounting for special methods in object-oriented class cohesion measurement, Journal of Software, 2013, Vol. 8. No. 2, pp. 327-336.

J. Al Dallal, Incorporating transitive relations in low-level design-based class cohesion measurement, Software: Practice and Experience, 2013, Vol. 43. No. 6, pp. 685-704.

J. Al Dallal, Object-oriented class maintainability prediction using internal quality attributes, Information and Software Technology, 2013, Vol. 55, No. 11, pp. 2028-2048.

J. Al Dallal, The effects of incorporating special methods into cohesion measurement on class instantiation reuse-proneness prediction, IET Software, 2014, Vol. 8, No. 6, pp. 285-295.

J. Al Dallal, Theoretical Analysis of the effect of accounting for special methods in similarity-based cohesion measurement, International Conference on Computer and Information Engineering ICCIE 2014, Istanbul, Turkey, 2014, pp. 555-558.

J. Al Dallal, Theoretical exploration for the impact of accounting for special methods in connectivity-based cohesion measurement, XII International Conference on

Communication, Information and Computing Technology (ICCICT 2014), Istanbul, Turkey, 2014.

J. Al Dallal, Accounting for data encapsulation in the measurement of object-oriented class cohesion, Journal of Software: Evolution and Process, Vol. 27, No. 5, 2015, pp. 373-400.

J. Al Dallal, Empirical investigation of the impact of accounting for transitive relationships on lack-of-cohesion measurement, 7th European Conference of Computer Science (ECCS '16), Rome, Italy, 2016.

J. Al Dallal, Predicting move method refactoring opportunities in object-oriented code, Information and Software Technology, 2017, Vol. 92, pp. 105–120.

J. Al Dallal, Empirical exploration for the correlation between object-oriented class cohesion and inheritance, International Conference on Advanced Sciences and Technology (ICAT'17), Istanbul, Turkey, 2017.

J. Al Dallal, Empirical exploration of correlations between software design measures: a replication study, ICCSIT 2018: 20th International Conference on Computer Science and Information Technology, Rome, Italy, 2018, pp. 46-49.

J. Al Dallal, Predicting fault-proneness of reused object-oriented classes in software post-releases, Arabian Journal for Science and Engineering, Vol. 43, No. 12, 2018, pp. 7153-7166.

J. Al Dallal, Predicting object-oriented class fault-proneness: a replication study. Journal of Software, Vol. 13, No. 5, 2018, pp. 269-276.

J. Al Dallal, A categorization-based approach for predicting the fault-proneness of object-oriented classes in software post-releases, IET Software, 2020, Vol. 14, No. 5, pp. 525-534.

J. Al Dallal, Investigating the relationship between cohesion and inheritance quality attributes empirically, Proceeding of the

2nd Computer Applications & Technological Solutions Conference (CATS' 23), Kuwait, October 2023.

J. Al Dallal and A. Abdin, Empirical evaluation of the impact of object-oriented code refactoring on quality attributes: a systematic literature review, IEEE Transactions on Software Engineering, Vol. 44, No. 1, 2018, pp. 44-69.

J. Al Dallal, H. Abdulsalam, M. AlMarzouq, A. Selamat, Machine learning-based exploration of the impact of move method refactoring on object-oriented software quality attributes. Arabian Journal for Science and Engineering , 2024, Vol. 49, pp. 3867–3885.

J. Al Dallal, B. Alkhazi, Exploring the impact of alternatives of object-oriented cohesion measures on machine learning-based predictions of inheritance reusability, IEEE Access, 2024, Vol. 12, pp. 59252-159266.

J. Al Dallal and L. Briand, An object-oriented high-level design-based class cohesion metric, Information and Software Technology, 2010, Vol. 52, No. 12, pp. 1346-1361.

J. Al Dallal and L. Briand, A Precise method-method interaction-based cohesion metric for object-oriented classes, ACM Transactions on Software Engineering and Methodology (TOSEM), 2012, Vol. 21, No. 2, pp. 8:1-8:34.

J. Al Dallal and S. Morasca, Predicting object-oriented class reuse-proneness using internal quality attributes, Empirical Software Engineering, Vol. 19, No. 4, 2014, pp. 775-821.

J. Al Dallal and S. Morasca, Investigating the impact of fault data completeness over time on predicting class fault-proneness, Information and Software Technology, Vol. 95, 2018, pp. 86-105.

L. Badri and M. Badri, A Proposal of a new class cohesion criterion: an empirical study, Journal of Object Technology, 2004, Vol. 3, No. 4, pp. 145-159.

J. Bieman and B. Kang, Cohesion and reuse in an object-oriented system, Proceedings of the 1995 Symposium on

Software reusability, Seattle, Washington, United States, 1995, pp. 259-262.

C. Bonja and E. Kidanmariam, Metrics for class cohesion and similarity between methods, Proceedings of the 44th Annual ACM Southeast Regional Conference, Melbourne, Florida, 2006, pp. 91-95.

L. C. Briand, J. Daly, and J. Wust, A unified framework for cohesion measurement in object-oriented systems, Empirical Software Engineering, 1998, Vol. 3, No. 1, pp. 65-117.

H. S. Chae, Y. R. Kwon, and D. Bae, A cohesion measure for object-oriented classes, Software—Practice & Experience, 2000, Vol. 30, No. 12, pp.1405-1431.

S.R. Chidamber and C.F. Kemerer, Towards a Metrics Suite for Object-Oriented Design, Object-Oriented Programming Systems, Languages and Applications (OOPSLA), Special Issue of SIGPLAN Notices, 1991, Vol. 26, No. 10, pp. 197-211.

S.R. Chidamber and C.F. Kemerer, A Metrics suite for object Oriented Design, IEEE Transactions on Software Engineering, 1994, Vol. 20, No. 6, pp. 476-493.

S. Counsell, S. Swift, and J. Crampton, The interpretation and utility of three cohesion metrics for object-oriented design, ACM Transactions on Software Engineering and Methodology (TOSEM), 2006, Vol. 15, No. 2, pp.123-149.

J. Devore, Probability and Statistics for Engineering and the Sciences, Cengage Learning, 8 edition, 2011.

DrJava, http://sourceforge.net/projects/drjava/, accessed in October 2025.

Eclipse, http://www.eclipse.org/, accessed in October 2025.

L. Fernández, and R. Peña, A sensitive metric of class cohesion, International Journal of Information Theories and Applications, 2006, Vol. 13, No. 1, pp. 82-91.

FreeMind, https://freemind.sourceforge.io/wiki/index.php/Main_Page , accessed in October 2025.

GanttProject, http://sourceforge.net/projects/ganttproject/, October 2025

B. Henderson-sellers, Object-Oriented Metrics Measures of Complexity, Prentice-Hall, 1996.

W. Hines, D. Montgomery, D. Goldsman, and C. Borror, *Probability and statistics in engineering*, 4th edition, John Wiley & Sons Inc., 2003.

M. Hitz and B. Montazeri, Measuring coupling and cohesion in object oriented systems, Proceedings of the International Symposium on Applied Corporate Computing, 1995, pp. 25-27.

Illusion, http://sourceforge.net/projects/aoi/, October 2025.

JabRef, http://sourceforge.net/projects/jabref/, October 2025

JHotDraw, http://sourceforge.net/projects/jhotdraw/, accessed in October 2025.

W. Li and S.M. Henry, Maintenance metrics for the object oriented paradigm. In Proceedings of 1st International Software Metrics Symposium, Baltimore, MD, 1993, pp. 52-60.

Openbravo, http://sourceforge.net/projects/openbravopos, October 2025.

W. Rosenkrantz, Introduction to Probability and Statistics for Science, Engineering, and Finance, Chapman and Hall/CRC, 1 edition, 2008.

B. Xu and Y. Zhou, Comments on 'A cohesion measure for object-oriented classes' by H. S. Chae, Y. R. Kwon and D. H. Bae (Softw. Pract. Exper. 2000, 30: 1405-1431), Software—Practice & Experience, 2001, Vol. 31, No. 14, pp. 1381-1388.

B. Xu and Y. Zhou, More comments on 'A cohesion measure for object-oriented classes' by H. S. Chae, Y. R. Kwon and D.

H. Bae (Softw. Pract. Exper. 2000, 30: 1405-1431), Software—Practice & Experience, 2003, Vol. 33, No. 6, pp.583-588.

X. Yang, Research on Class Cohesion Measures, M.S. Thesis, Department of Computer Science and Engineering, Southeast University, 2002.

INDEX

A

Absence of cohesion, 28, 30, 31, 45, 116
Access methods, 128, 130, 131, 132, 133, 134, 136, 137, 138, 139, 140, 141, 142, 143, 144, 145, 147, 150, 152, 153
Adaptability, 7
All-simple-paths tree, 52, 53, 55
Applicability, 8, 85, 99, 102, 127, 146, 157
Art of Illusion, 100, 121, 123, 143
Attribute-attribute interaction, 21
Attribute-method interaction, 21, 22
Average absolute change, 151

B

Bibliographical databases, 100, 144
Binary codes, 113, 118
Binary files, 113

C

Calendaring, 100, 143
CAMC, 27, 29, 62, 63, 85, 97, 102, 105, 116, 118, 122, 125, 141, 142, 152, 154
CBMC, 27, 46, 47, 48, 77, 78, 79, 139, 140, 141, 152, 154
CC, 27, 38, 39, 68, 69, 85, 90, 92, 102, 104, 109, 116, 117, 120, 122, 125, 134, 135, 136, 146, 152, 154
Class cohesion, 8, 9, 25, 27, 45, 50, 58, 59, 60, 82, 84, 85, 90, 105, 106, 110, 111, 116, 126, 127, 128, 157, 158, 159, 160, 161
Class cohesion measures, 59, 83, 105, 127
Class measures, 27
Class members, 9, 25, 45, 59
Class model, 25, 44, 61, 65, 66, 67
Class modeling, 13
Class quality, 101, 126
Class reference graph, 45
Class-representative graph, 132, 139, 140
Coh, 27, 28, 60, 61, 63, 68, 85, 95, 96, 102, 104, 108, 116, 125, 137, 146, 152, 154
Cohesion interactions, 62, 63, 64

Cohesion level, 104, 110, 124, 129
Cohesion measure, 8, 9, 25, 27, 45, 50, 58, 59, 60, 61, 82, 85, 86, 87, 89, 90, 91, 93, 94, 98, 102, 104, 105, 106, 108, 110, 111, 112, 113, 115, 124, 126, 127, 128, 131, 143, 144, 153, 160, 161, 162
Cohesion measurement, 8, 9, 46, 105, 110, 112, 113, 114, 120, 124, 125, 126, 127, 128, 130, 131, 132, 133, 134, 137, 139, 140, 144, 149, 153, 154, 158, 159, 161
Cohesion properties, 9, 59, 68, 69, 84, 86, 87
Cohesive interaction, 13, 14, 15, 16, 17, 60, 61, 63, 64, 65, 66, 67, 68, 69, 71, 73, 74, 75, 76, 78, 79, 80, 82, 88, 89, 90, 91, 92, 93, 94, 95
Cohesive modules, 60, 63, 68, 70, 73, 77, 87, 91, 92, 93, 94, 95, 96, 97, 98, 99
Cohesive modules property, 68, 70, 73, 77, 87, 91, 92, 93, 94, 95, 96, 98, 99
Common attribute, 30, 31, 32, 62, 63, 64, 68, 69, 70, 71, 73, 74, 104, 135, 137
Completeness, 7, 160
Connected components, 45, 75
Connectivity, 44, 45, 46, 47, 49, 76, 77, 157, 158
Connectivity factor, 46, 47, 49
Connectivity measure, 44, 45, 76, 77
Connectivity pattern, 44
Connectivity-based measures, 44
Constant weight, 111, 112, 113, 121, 124, 126, 127
Constructor, 104, 128, 129, 130, 131, 132, 133, 134, 135, 136, 137, 138, 139, 140, 141, 142, 143, 144, 145, 146, 150, 152, 153, 154
Constructor method, 104, 132, 134, 135, 137
Correlations, 101, 159
Cut set, 47, 48, 49
Cyclic reference, 106

D

DAT, 20, 21, 22
Data encapsulation, 9, 105, 127, 159
DC_D, 27, 36, 37, 66, 67, 85, 90, 137, 138, 146, 152, 154
DC_I, 27, 37, 38, 67, 85, 90, 137, 138, 146, 152, 154
DE, 105, 110, 112, 114, 120, 124, 125, 126, 127
Degree of Cohesion, 36, 37
Degree of connectivity, 44
Degree of similarity, 125, 142
Delegation method, 128, 129, 130, 144, 153, 154
Denominator, 61, 65, 66, 67, 69, 71, 74, 77, 125, 126, 133

Descriptive statistics, 119, 120, 121, 122, 123, 125, 145, 149, 150
Design phase, 28
Destructors, 128, 129, 130, 144, 153, 154
Developers, 7, 85
Development phase, 27
Direct Attribute-Type (DAT) matrix, *see* DAT
Direct Method Invocation (DMI) matrix, *see* DMI
Direct Method-Attribute (DMA) matrix, *see* DMA
Direct Method-Method Connectivity (DMMC), *see* DMMC
Direct Method-Method Connectivity (DMMC) graph, *see* DMMC graph
Direct Parameter-Type (DPT) matrix, *see* DPT
Direct relations, 129, 131
Directly connected, 32, 33, 35, 36, 37, 50, 138
Directly referenced, 17
Discriminative power, 157
Disjoint components, 45, 75, 76
Disjoint graphs, 76
Disjoint reference graph, 44
Disjointed components, 133
Distinct attributes, 28, 29, 104, 113, 125, 130, 133, 134, 135, 136, 137
Distinct parameter types, 23, 29, 42, 86, 98, 100, 113
Distinct types of parameters, 141
DMA, 16, 18, 28, 29, 30, 31, 32, 38, 39, 40, 108, 109
DMI, 18, 19, 20
DMMC, 13, 14, 30, 31, 32, 45
DMMC graph, 13, 14, 30, 31, 32, 45
DPT, 23, 24, 29, 42, 108
DrJava, 116, 120, 123, 161

E

Eclipse, 116, 119, 122, 123, 161
Editing system, 143
Elementary graph, 48, 49
Empirical analysis, 110, 143, 150
Empirical results, 129
Empirical study(ies), 86, 101, 110, 112, 113, 124, 127, 144, 146, 160
Empirical validation, 86, 99
Encapsulated attribute, 105, 106, 107, 127
Encapsulated data, 106, 110, 124, 126, 127
Encapsulation, 104, 110, 127, 128, 154
Excel, 113
Experiment, 122

F

Fault repositories, 100, 144
Fault-proneness, 124, 159, 160
FG, 53, 55, 56
Freemind, 120, 122, 123, 143, 162
Fully connected, 53, 82, 139
Functionality(ies), 128, 154

G

GanttProject, 100, 143, 162
Getter, 128, 130, 141, 142, 144
Glue methods, 46, 47, 139
Graph connectivity, 9, 27, 58
Graph-based models, 13
Graphical application, 100, 143

H

Hamming Distance, 42
High-level design, *see* HLD
HLD, 8, 27, 29, 42, 43, 86
HTML, 100, 143

I

IAT, 21, 22, 23, 43, 44, 74
ICBMC, 27, 47, 49, 50, 79, 80
IMA, 16, 17, 18, 32, 33, 35, 36, 37, 38, 40, 41, 42, 71
IMI, 20, 22
IMMC, 14, 45, 46
Implicit access, 127
Independent sets of samples, 116, 148
Indirect Attribute-Type (IAT) matrix, *see* IAT
Indirect Method Invocation (IMI) matrix, *see* IMI
Indirect Method-Attribute (IMA) matrix, *see* IMA
Indirect Method-Method Connectivity (IMMC), *see* IMMC
Indirect Parameter-Type (IPT) matrix, *see* IPT
Indirect relations, 129, 131
Inheritance, 105, 158, 159, 160
IPT, 23, 24

J

JabRef, 100, 143, 162
Java, 13, 14, 15, 16, 17, 19, 34, 39, 47, 49, 55, 56, 100, 104, 107, 109, 113, 118, 143, 144
Java Development Kit (JDK), *see* JDK
JDK, 118
JHotDraw, 113, 120, 123, 162

K

KLOC, 100

L

lack of cohesion, 28, 45, 89, 90, 91, 93, 94, 95, 98, 99, 131, 153
Large-scale systems, 127
Large-size-system, 113
LCC, 27, 33, 35, 36, 37, 38, 65, 66, 85, 90, 104, 137, 138, 146, 152, 154

$LCOM_{CK1}$, 27, 30, 31, 63, 64, 85, 90, 91, 104, 131, 132, 150, 152, 154
$LCOM_{CK2}$, 27, 31, 32, 64, 65, 85, 90, 91, 104, 132, 152, 154
$LCOM_{H}$, 27, 28, 29, 62, 85, 87, 93, 94, 95, 102, 104, 116, 117, 125, 133, 134, 146, 152, 154
$LCOM_{HM}$, 27, 45, 46, 76, 77, 86, 104, 132, 133, 152, 154
$LCOM_{L}$, 27, 45, 75, 76, 86, 104, 132, 133, 152, 154
Lines of code, 100, 113
LLD, 8, 27, 28, 30, 31, 32, 33, 36, 37, 38, 39, 40, 45, 46, 47, 50, 52, 86
Loose Class Cohesion, 33
Low-level design, *see* LLD
LSCC, 27, 40, 41, 70, 71, 72, 86, 104, 109, 116, 125, 134, 136, 142, 151, 152, 154

M

MAC, 15, 16, 46, 47, 48, 49, 50, 51, 52, 53, 54, 55, 56, 57, 77, 78, 79, 80, 81, 82
Machine learning, 8, 11, 160
Maintainability, 7, 8, 85, 124, 158
Manageability, 85
Matrix-based models, 13, 25
Mean cohesion values, 110, 117, 125
Mean values, 116, 118, 125, 147, 152
Measure applicability, 9
Medium-sized system, 113
Merged class, 60, 63, 64, 65, 71, 73, 74, 78, 79, 81, 87, 91, 92, 94
Method invocation, 13, 18, 20, 90, 138
Method measures, 27
Method pairs, 23, 30, 31, 32, 33, 38, 109, 132
Method-Attribute Connectivity, 15
Method-Attribute Connectivity (MAC) graph, 15
Method-attribute interactions, 8, 9, 25, 77, 79, 80
Method-Method Connectivity, 13, 14
Method-method interaction, 9, 21, 23, 24, 25, 71, 74, 160, 90
MMAC, 27, 43, 44, 73, 74, 75, 142, 152, 154
MMI, 90, 91, 92
Modularity, 104
Monotonic, 125
Monotonicity, 60, 63, 69, 70, 71, 74, 82, 91, 92, 93, 94, 95, 96, 97, 98, 99
MS Project, 100, 143

N

NHD, 27, 42, 72, 73, 85, 87, 98, 99, 105, 116, 118, 120, 122, 125, 126, 141, 142, 146, 152, 154
Non-negativity, 60, 68, 69, 71, 73, 77, 79, 80, 81, 90, 91, 92, 93, 94, 95, 96, 97, 98, 99
Non-parametric statistical technique, 116
Non-peer access method, 134, 136, 137, 138
Nonspecial methods, 46, 47, 130, 135, 136, 138, 146, 150
Non-special methods, 138
Normal distribution, 116, 120
Normal methods, 46, 51
Normalization, 60, 68, 69, 71, 73, 77, 79, 80, 81, 90, 91, 92, 93, 94, 95, 96, 97, 98, 99
Normalization property, 71, 73, 77, 79, 80, 81, 90, 91, 92, 93, 94, 95
Null and maximum value property, 63, 71, 73, 74, 78, 79, 80
Null hypothesis, 112, 118, 120, 121, 124
Null value and maximum value property, 81, 91, 92, 93, 94, 95
Numerator, 61, 65, 66, 67, 69, 71, 74, 77, 125, 126, 133

O

Object attribute, 106, 107
Object type, 105, 106, 107, 110, 112, 113, 114, 115, 116, 117, 118, 124, 125, 126, 127
Object-oriented paradigm, 128
Object-oriented program, 104
Object-oriented programming, 128
Object-oriented systems, 8, 27, 85, 90, 161
OL_2, 51, 152
OL_n, 27, 50, 80, 81, 140, 141, 154
OO programming, 104, 106, 110
OO programming language, 104
Openbravo, 100, 143, 162
Open-source libraries, 118
Open-source software, 100, 143
Open-source systems, 100, 144

P

Pair of data sets, 116, 121
Pair(s) of methods, 24, 30, 31, 32, 33, 36, 37, 38, 39, 40, 41, 42, 43, 44, 62, 63, 68, 69, 70, 71, 73, 74, 90, 92, 98, 104, 106, 109, 113, 125, 126, 131, 134, 137, 141
Paired z-test, 148, 149, 150
Parameter agreement, 42
Parameter type, 9, 21, 22, 23, 24, 25, 28, 62, 73, 85, 86, 98,

105, 110, 113, 116, 125, 126, 127, 141, 142
Path Connectivity, 52
PCCC, 27, 52, 55, 56, 81, 82, 140, 152, 154
PDF, 100, 143
Peer access method, 136, 138
PMs, 105
Point-of-sale, 100, 144
Primitive attribute, 105
Primitive type, 104, 105, 106, 107, 108, 110, 115, 119, 127
Project managers, 7
Project scheduling application, 100
Project-scheduling, 143
p-value, 116, 118

Q

Qualitative, 129, 150, 153
Qualitative analysis, 129, 153
Quality assessment, 9
Quality attributes, 7, 8, 158, 159, 160
  External quality attributes, 7
  Internal quality attributes, 8

R

Recursive algorithm, 106, 121
Refactoring, 11, 154, 158, 159, 160
Reference graph, 44, 52
Reference type, 104, 127
Resource management, 100, 143
Return type, 21, 142, 144
Reusability, 7, 124, 160, 161

S

SCOM, 27, 39, 40, 69, 70, 85, 90, 92, 102, 104, 109, 116, 123, 125, 136, 137, 146, 152, 154
Sensitive Class Cohesion, 39
Setter, 128, 130, 141, 142, 144
Shapiro-Wilk normality test, 116, 120
Shared attributes, 30, 63, 68, 104, 105, 127, 134, 136
Signatures of the methods, 125
Significance of the change, 118
Significance threshold, 116, 148
Similarity(ies), 30, 38, 39, 40, 41, 43, 44, 68, 69, 92, 109, 134, 135, 136, 137, 142, 158, 161
Similarity degree, 30, 113
Similarity-based measures, 125
Simple path, 52, 53, 54, 55, 56, 81, 82, 140
Software artifacts, 8
Software developers, 85
Software engineering, 7, 9
Software engineers, 8, 126
Software practitioners, 143
Software quality, 7, 9, 143, 160
Source code, 8, 100, 144
Special method, 9, 47, 48, 128, 130, 131, 135, 137, 138, 143,

145, 146, 148, 151, 152, 153, 154, 157, 158
Standard deviation, 145, 148
Statistically significant, 148
Strength, 50, 130, 140
Strength of an attribute, 140
String, 21, 119
Studio system, 100, 143

T

TCC, 27, 32, 33, 36, 37, 65, 85, 90, 104, 137, 138, 146, 152, 154
Testability, 7
Text file, 113
Theoretical validation, 59, 60, 83
Tight Class Cohesion, 32
Touchscreens, 144, 100
Transitive attribute references, 25
Transitive DE, 105
Transitive method invocations, 25
Transitively connected, 33, 35, 37, 52, 137, 138
Transitively referenced, 17
Tree path, 56

U

Understandability, 7, 8, 85
Undirected edges, 13, 14, 15
Undirected graph, 13, 14, 15
Unrelated classes, 61, 63, 64, 65, 66, 67, 68, 70, 71, 74, 76, 77, 78, 79, 81, 82
Unrelated modules, 60, 78, 79, 81

W

Weight assignment, 105, 106, 107, 112, 113, 115, 121, 124, 126, 127
Wilcoxon paired test, 116, 118, 120
Wilcoxon test, 121

Z

Z value, 148
z-test analysis, 151

www.ingramcontent.com/pod-product-compliance
Lightning Source LLC
LaVergne TN
LVHW022044200926
848481LV00003B/783
* 9 7 8 1 7 7 7 9 0 2 5 0 6 *